Portrait of Asia

A Collection of Photographs

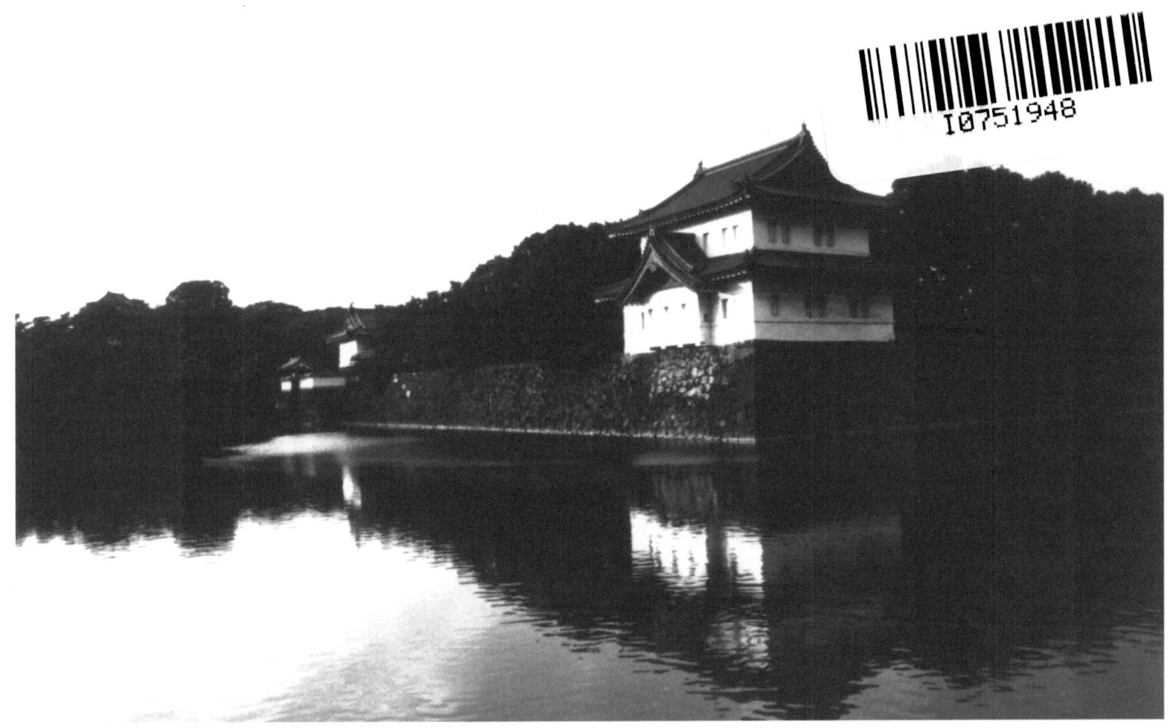

Photography and Text by

Mkemo Zaire London

Portrait of Asia
A Collection of Photographs

Photography

Printed in United States of America

ISBN: 978-0-6151-4834-2

Prints from this book are on sale at the following:
www.mkemolondon.com

For more information email: ml@mkemolondon.com

Cover: The Great Buddha (Daibutsu) in Kamakura, Japan
Previous page: Emperor's Palace in Tokyo, Japan

contents

In loving memory,
Sipho T. London and Sammie D. London
Thanks for always believing in me.

acknowledgements

There are many people who I would like to recognize that helped with the creation of this book. First, I would like to thank God; through him all things are possible. Niambi Sims, my heart, my love, my future wife, thanks for all your help, support and editing to see this book to completion. My Mother Cynthia London whose strength is a never changing constant in my life and the lives of everyone she touches. To my Grandmother Pauline London, who taught me wisdom, knowledge and strength; my sister Jewel Motley and her family, husband Winston and children; Jasmine, Winston and Akayla as well as sister Valetta Gregg and niece Valencia Gregg.

To my cousin Dominique London, whose advice, inspiration and sense of humor has been greatly appreciated, I cannot wait to read your books. I appreciate the support from the following people: my Uncle Woodrow Evans and the entire Evans family, the entire London family, my niece Amira Guy-Jones and the Guy family, Jason Oquendo, Harold DeLoach and family, Doris Sims, Adjua Sims-Copeland and Kwame Copeland.

To all my good friends from the US Navy; Daniel Mennuto, Tyrone Marsh, Adam Eastman and Kenyatta Joans; I learned so much about photography, art and the Navy. Thanks, for everything.

To my only brother Sipho London, there is not a day that goes by that I don't miss you and love you, this book is for you. My father Sammie London, Jr., I hope this book would have made you proud.

To all my relatives, rest in peace: Sammie London, Sr., Wayman London, William "Ike" London, Willie "Sugar" London, Joseph Evans, Sr., Joseph Evans, Jr., Tyrone Evans, Vinella Evans, Celester Moody, Howard Moody, Gwen Moody, Edison Clayton, Charity Clayton, and Prince and Eveliner Clayton.

To all who support my art. Peace.

introduction

I began my photographic journey in 1993 with a simple point and shoot camera while residing in my hometown of Philadelphia, Pennsylvania. I used to photograph friends, family and all that I encountered. It was not until 1998, while serving in the US Navy, visiting Pusan, South Korea; that I purchased a Canon AE1 manual camera. With mentoring and patience from my good friends Daniel Mennuto, Tyrone Marsh and Adam Eastman; I learned the technical practice of manual photography. Inspired by the artistry of Gordon Parks, Charles Moore, Herb Ritz and Annie Leibovitz, I bring you Portrait of Asia.

I was on a pilgrimage, photographing the beauty and mystery of Asia. I wanted these images as a personal journal of my travels. I chose 35mm black and white film as my format, because the black and white photograph is a medium that exposes truth in each subject captured. Along this journey, I decided to share my vision with the world in the form of this book. What resulted is a collection of photographs that captures a view into the urban and cultural life of Asia. The images range from subways and crowds, to the quiet moments of reflection found all over Asia.

This book is a snapshot of a people rich in tradition and culture. From the streets of Downtown Tokyo and Yokohama, Japan to Hong Kong and Thailand, as well as, the proud history of Hiroshima and the Great Buddha of Kamakura. Life in Japan, Thailand and Hong Kong was the motivation for this work

This collection of 35 black and white photographs, taken between 1998 and 2000, is divided into two sections; People and Places. People, represents the intimate portraits of the public as well as individuals I encountered as I made my way through Asia. Places, is made up of sites that represent the architectural, historical and urban landscape throughout this land. Each photograph is titled with the description, place and year.

Enjoy my photographic perspective of this magical place.

people

Monk, Yokosuka, Japan 1998

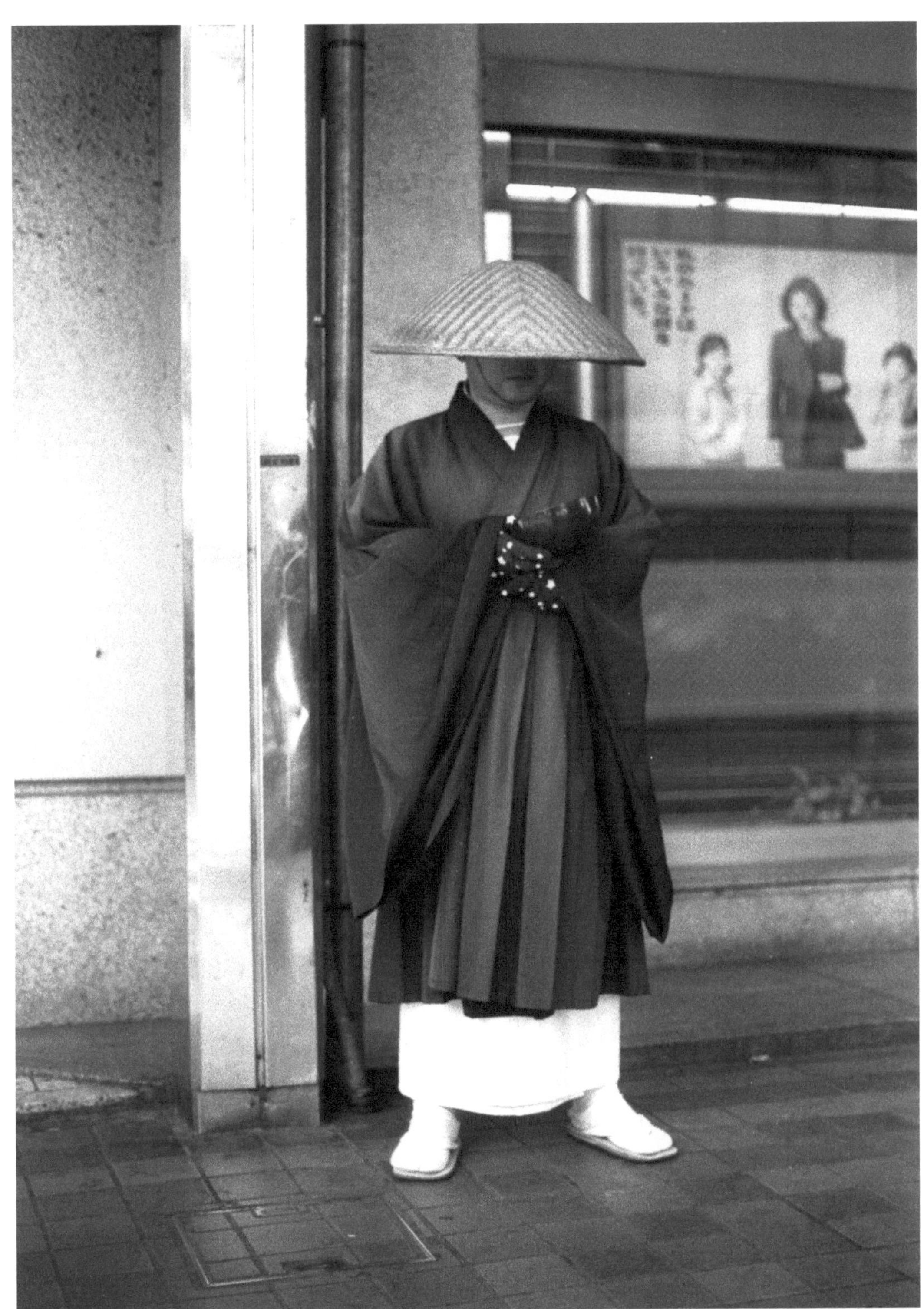

Cherry Blossom Festival, Yokosuka, Japan 1999

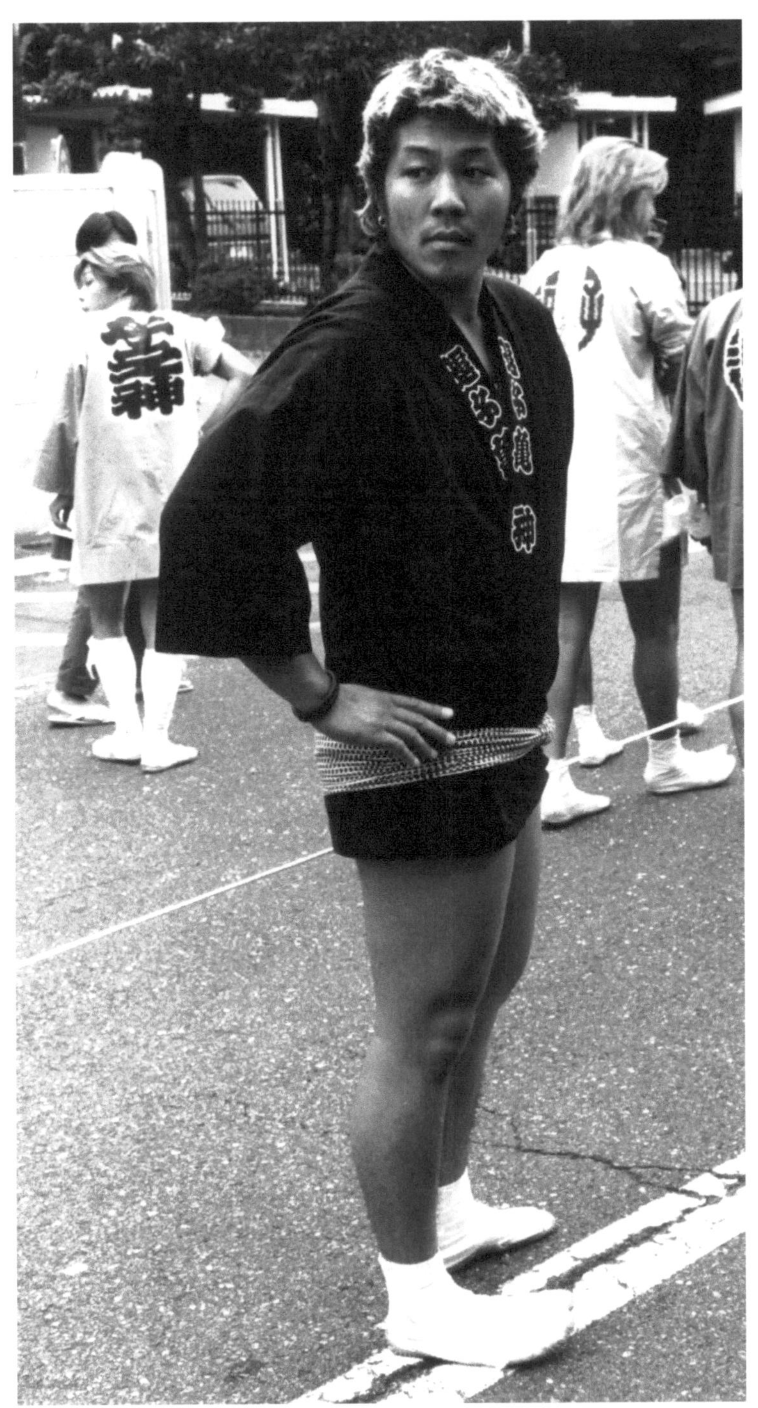

Thai Taxi Driver, Phuket, Thailand 1999

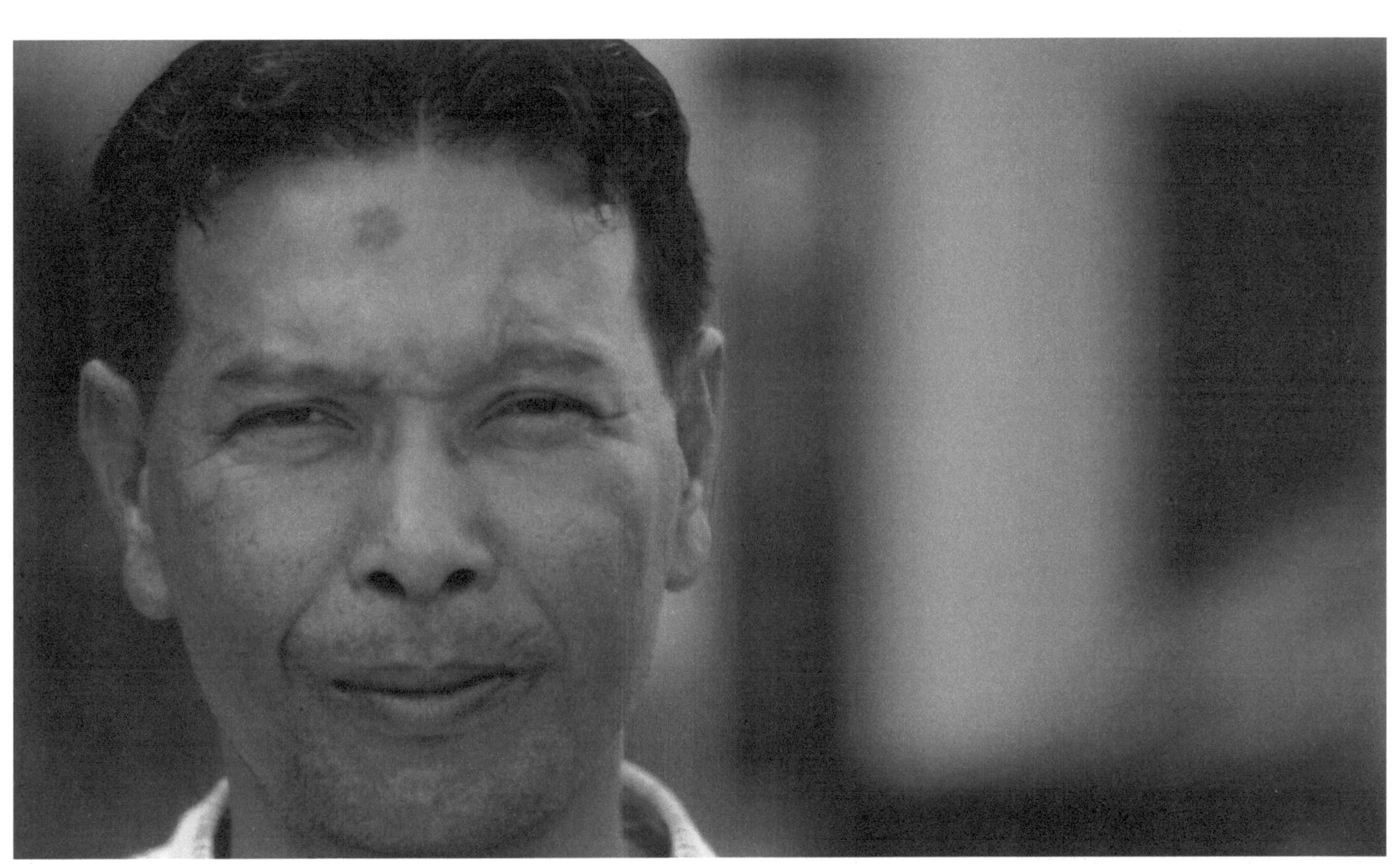

Woman in Thought, Hong Kong, China 1999

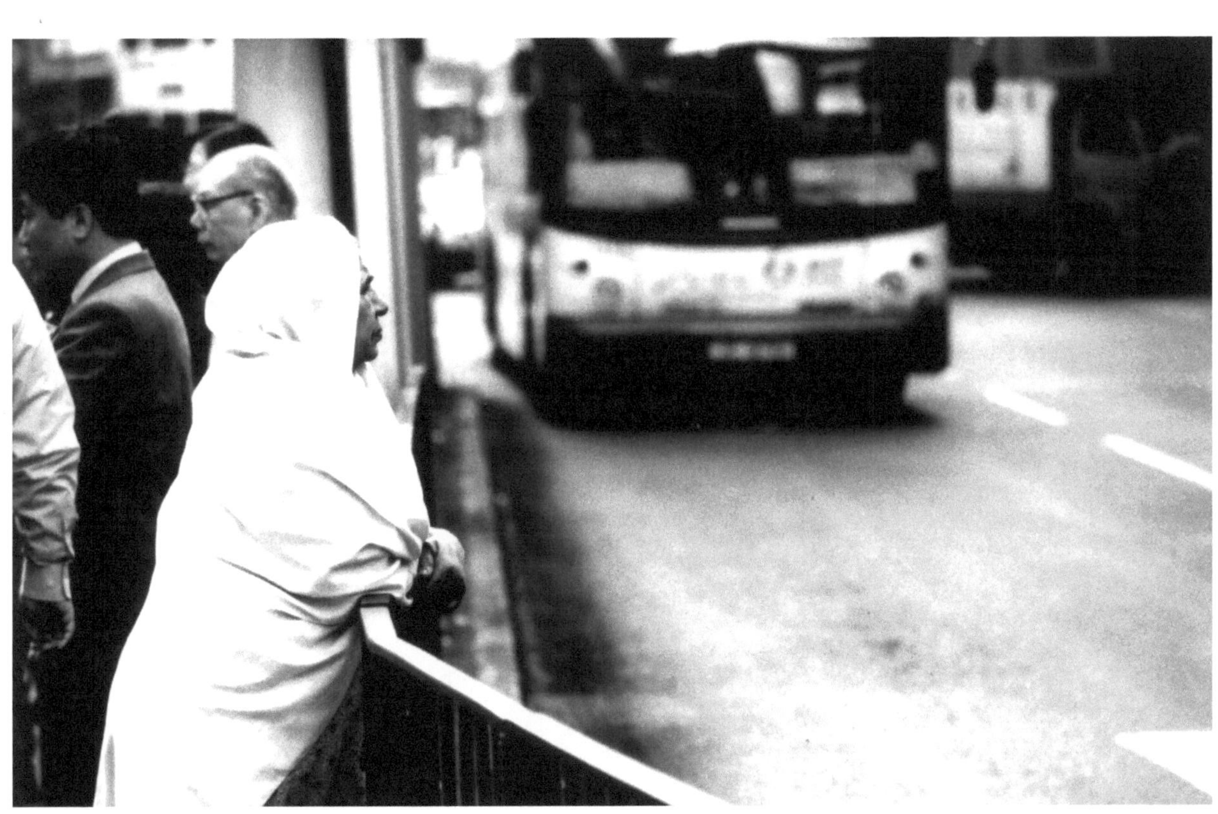

Young Lady, Yokosuka, Japan 1999

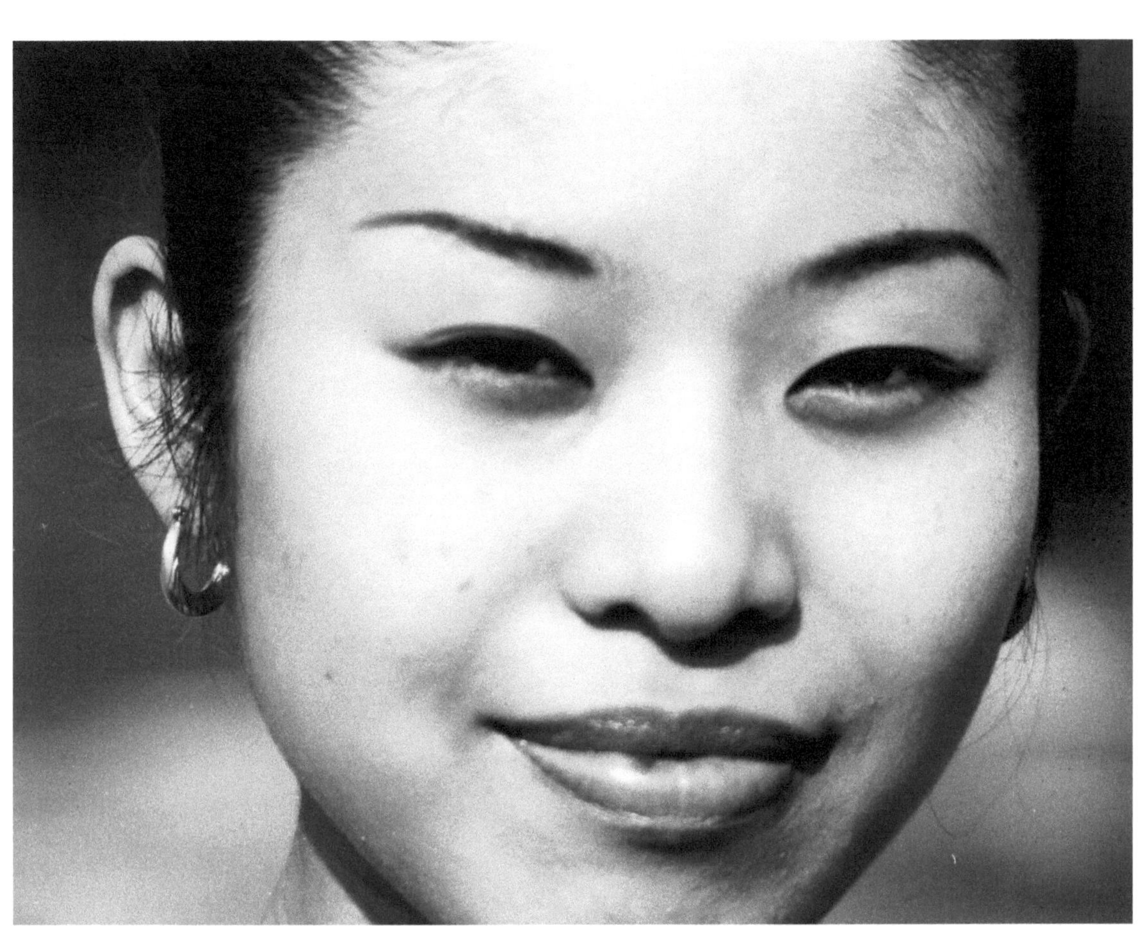

DJ Baby, Tokyo, Japan 1998

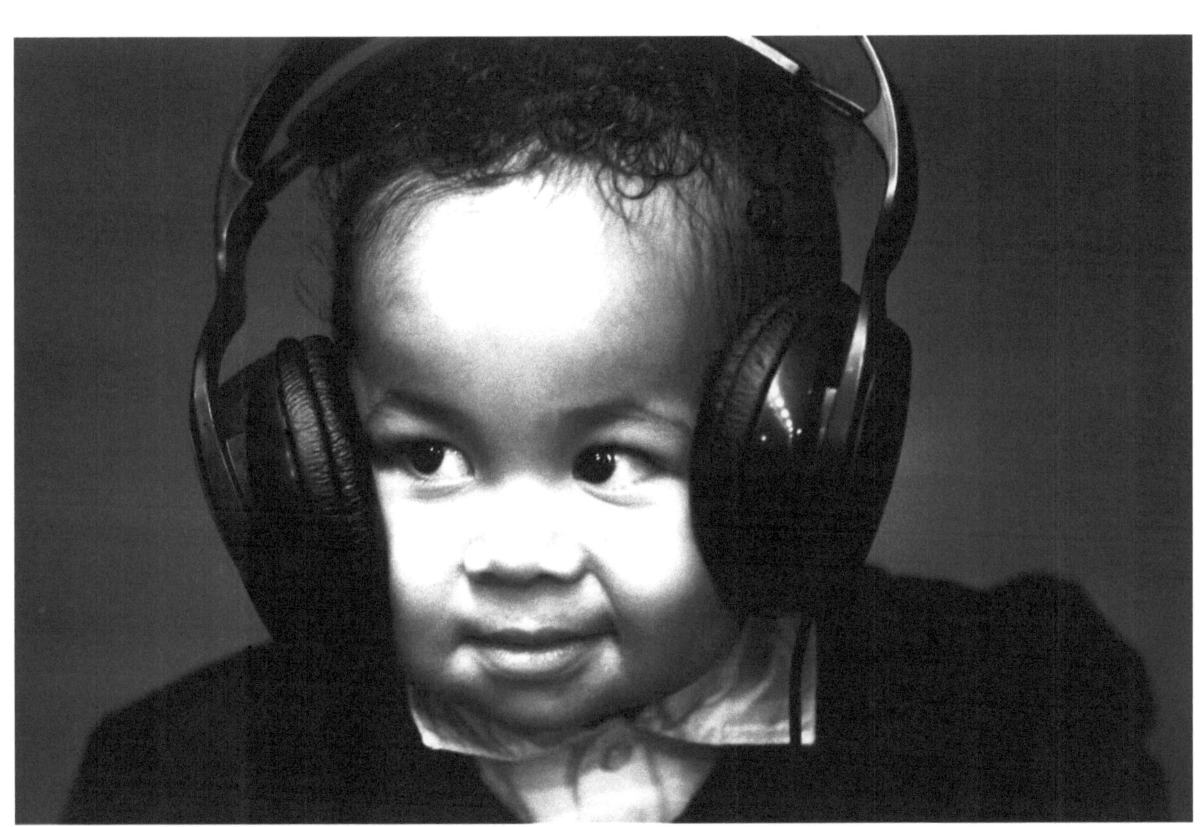

A child at the Tokyo Zoo, Ueno Park, Tokyo, Japan 2000

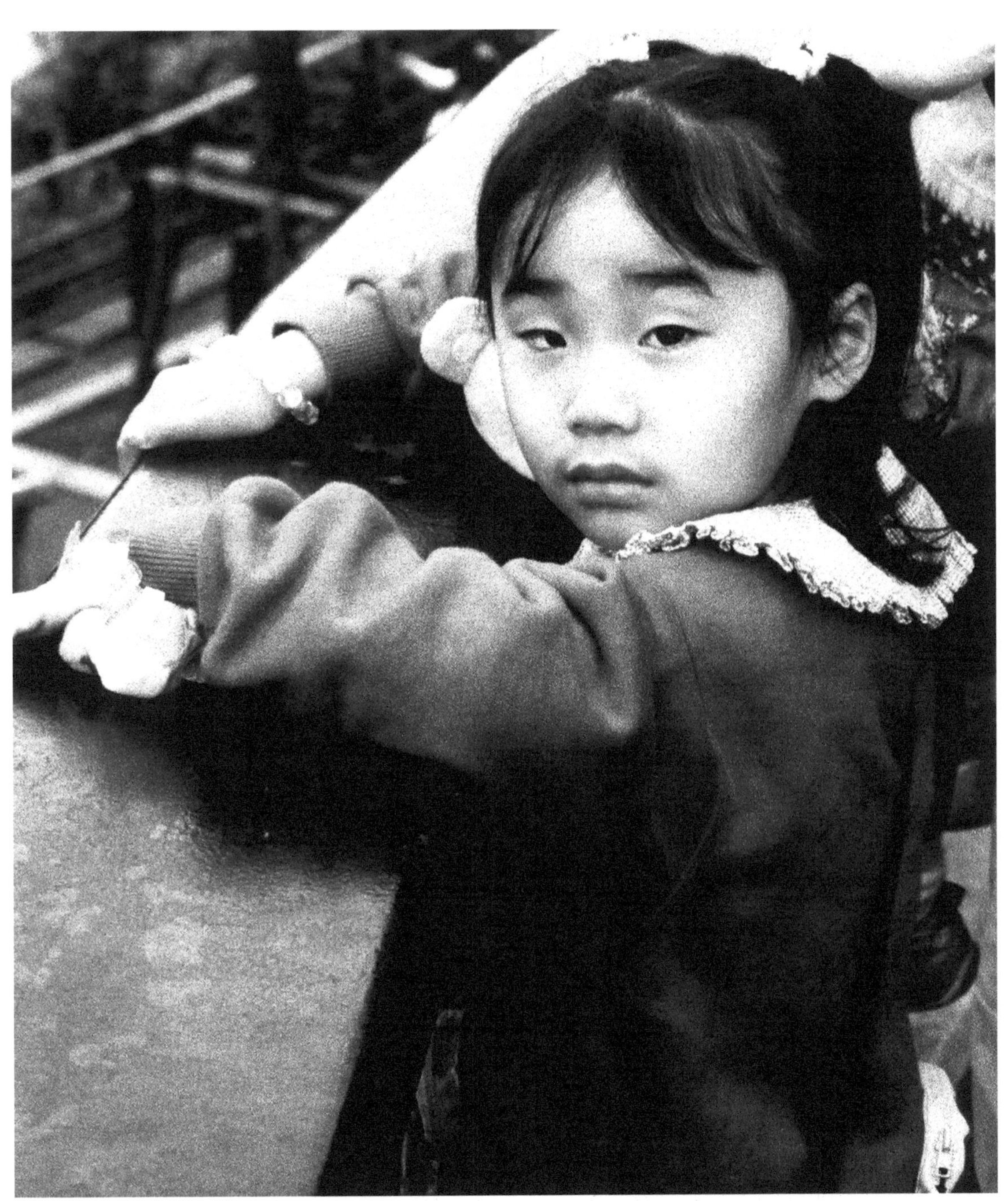

Children playing in Mikasa Park, Yokosuka, Japan 1998

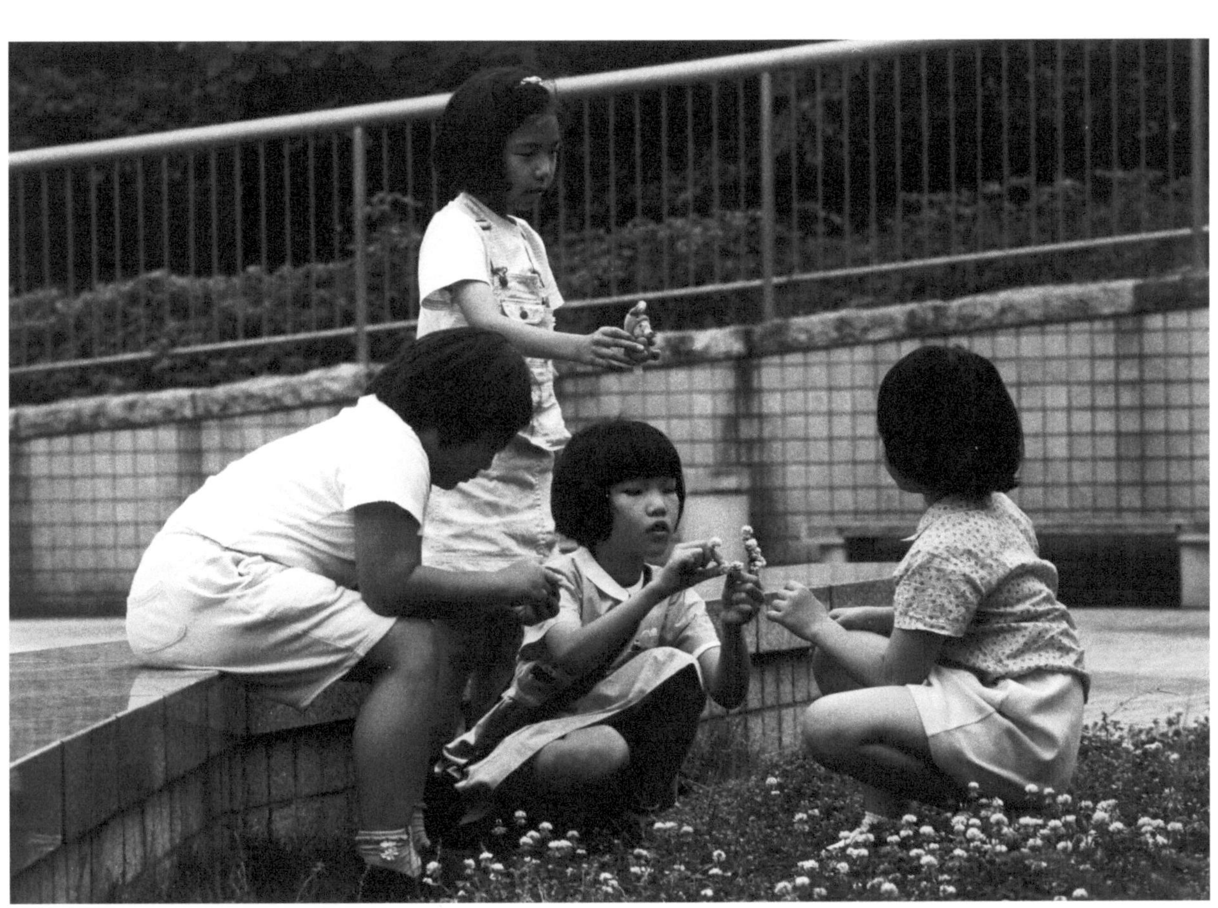

Laughing, Hong Kong, China 1999

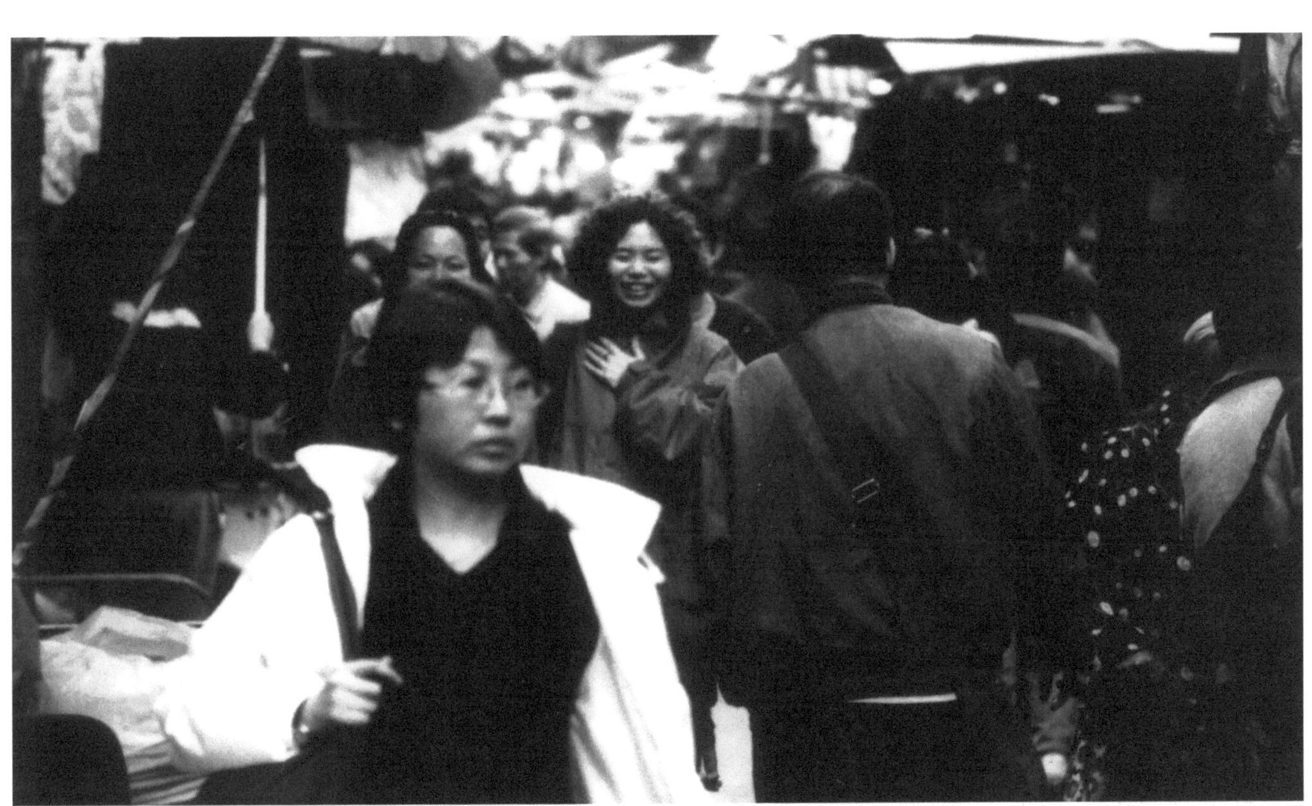

Yokosuka-Chou station on the Keihin Kyuko Line, Yokosuka, Japan 1998

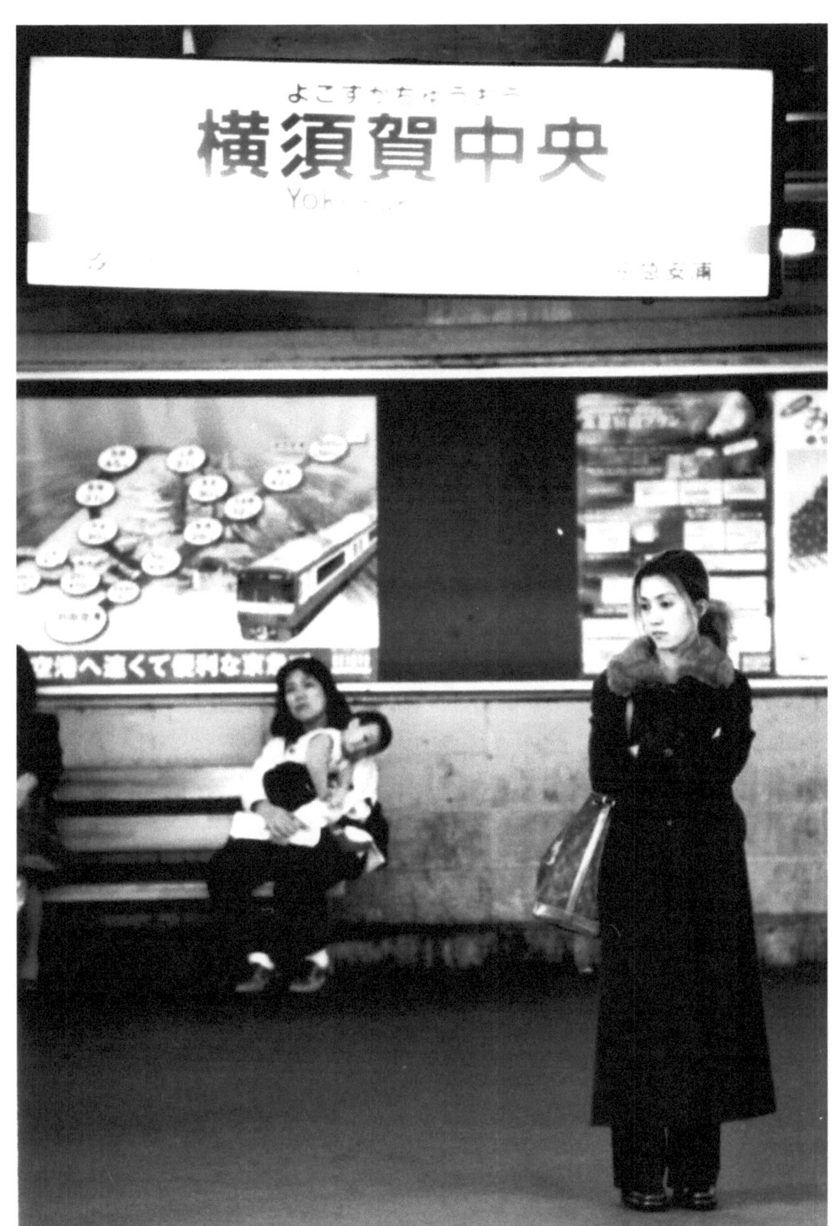
横須賀中央

Traveling, Yokosuka, Japan 1998

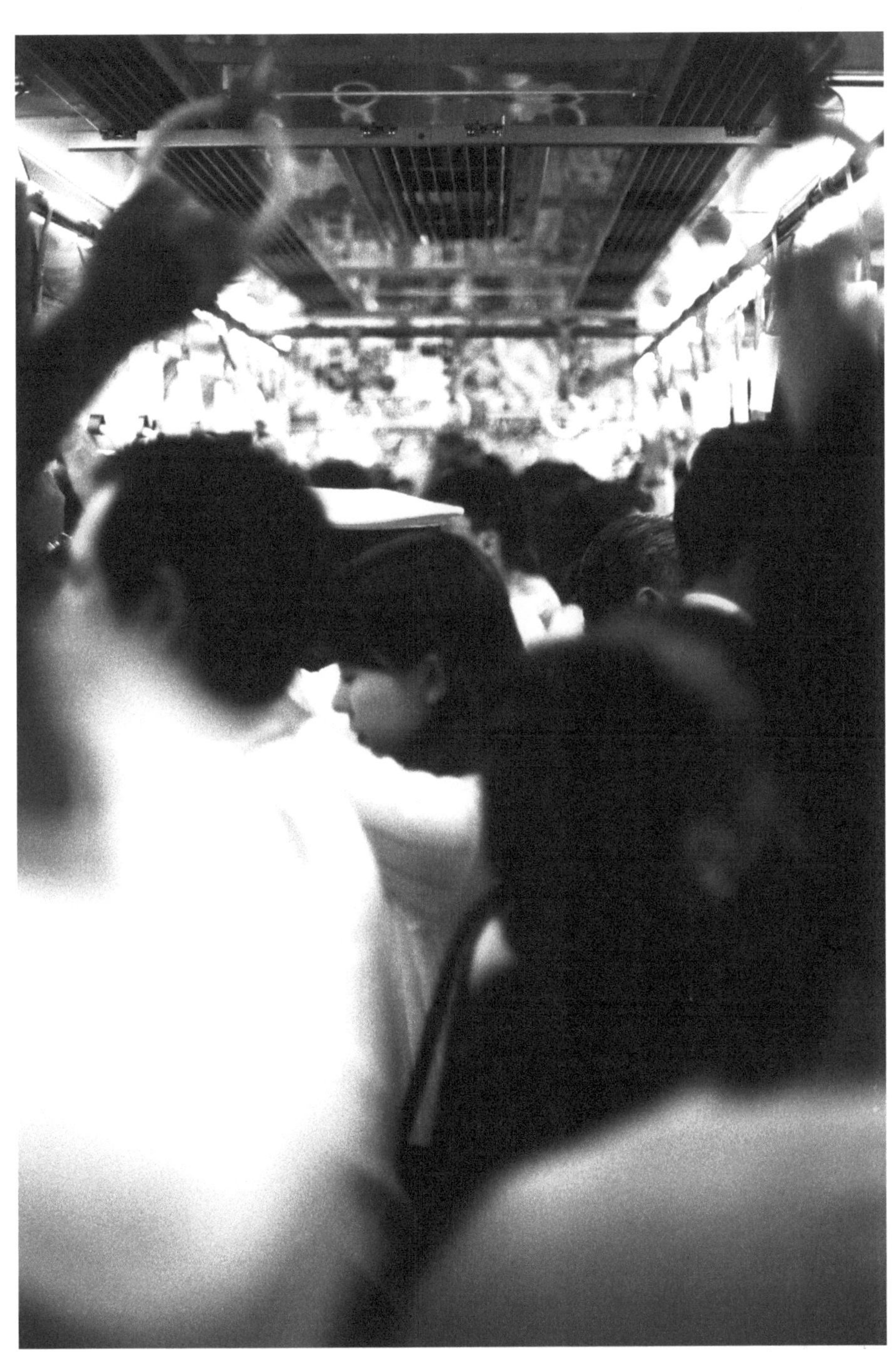

Reading, Tokyo, Japan 1999

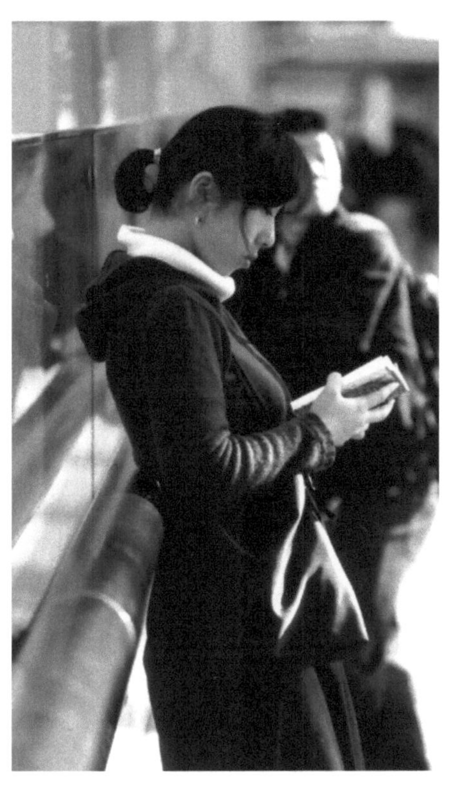

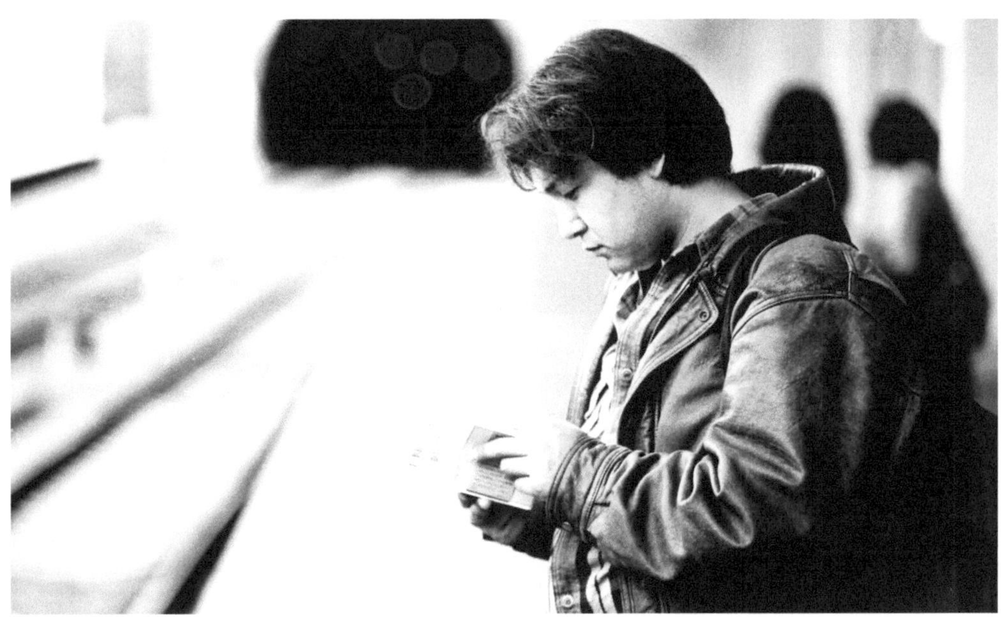

Friends, Tokyo, Japan 2000

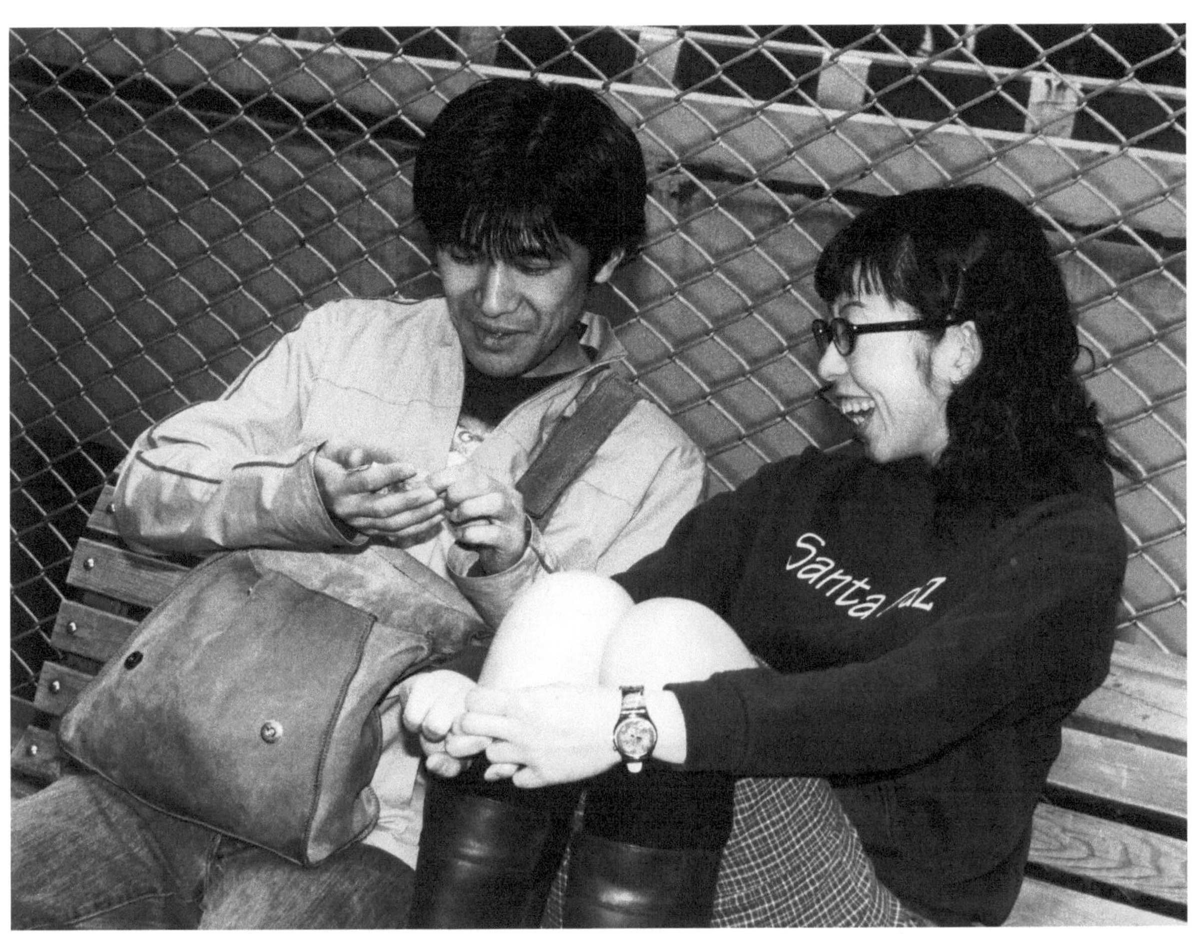

Thai Boxer, Phuket, Thailand 2000

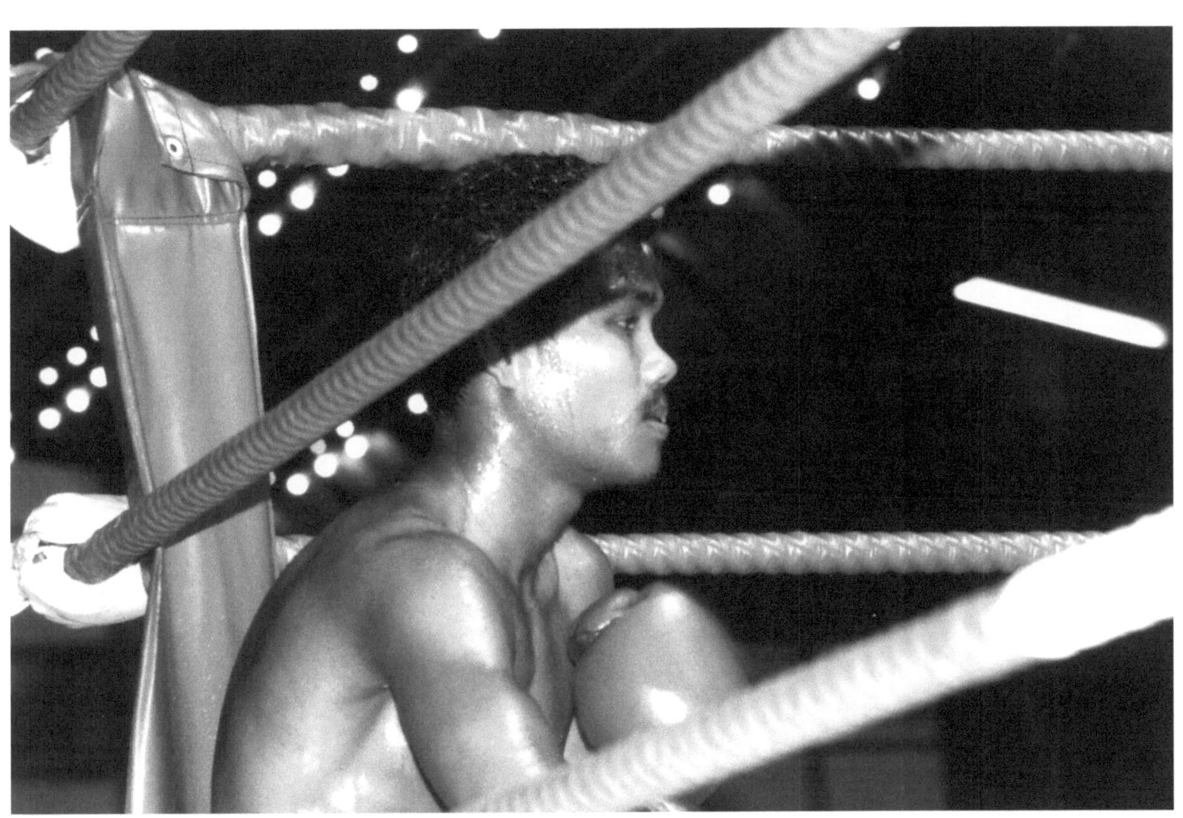

Thai Boxing, Phuket, Thailand 2000

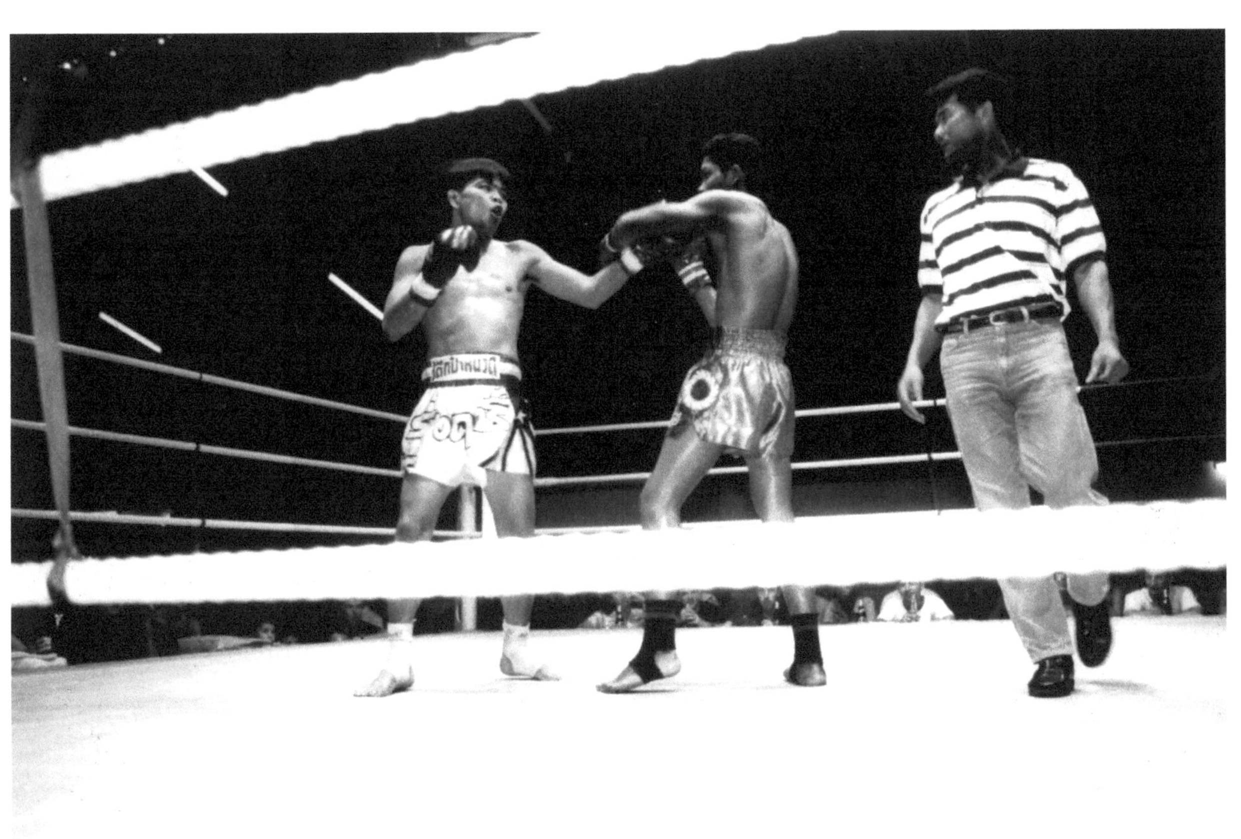

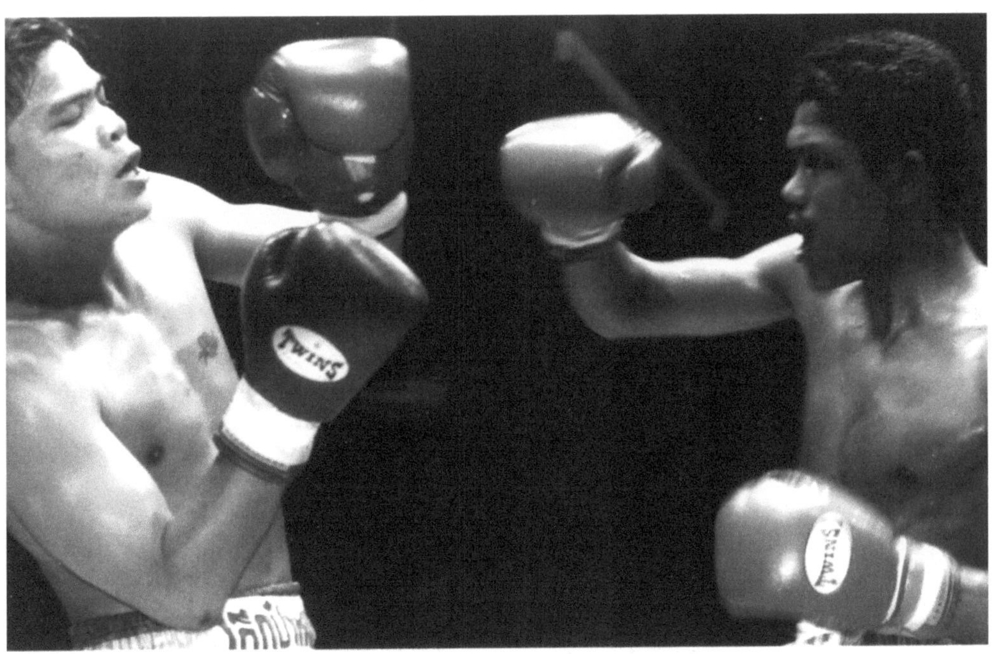
TWINS
TWINS

Rockin', Yokosuka, Japan 1999

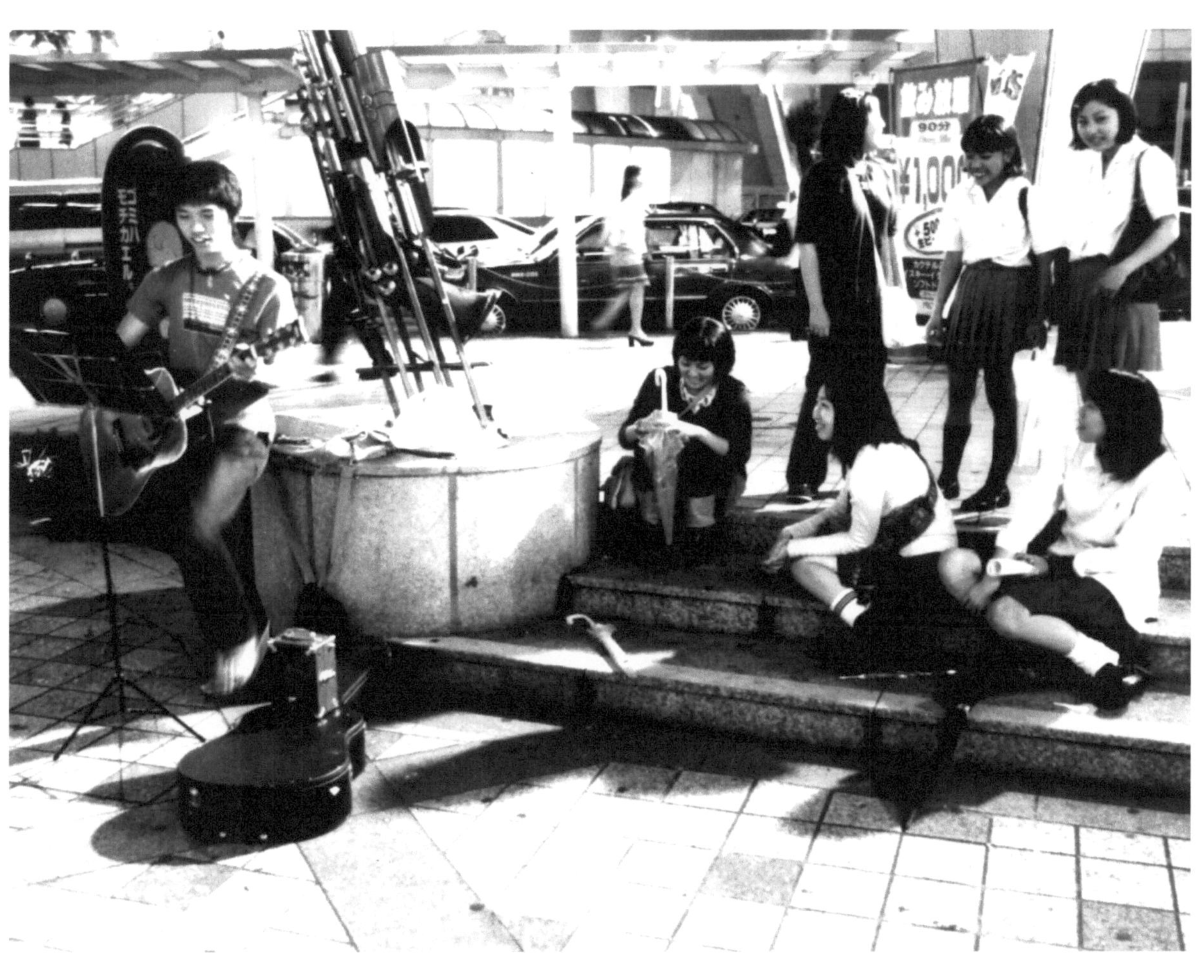

90分

Shibuya Night, Tokyo, Japan 1999

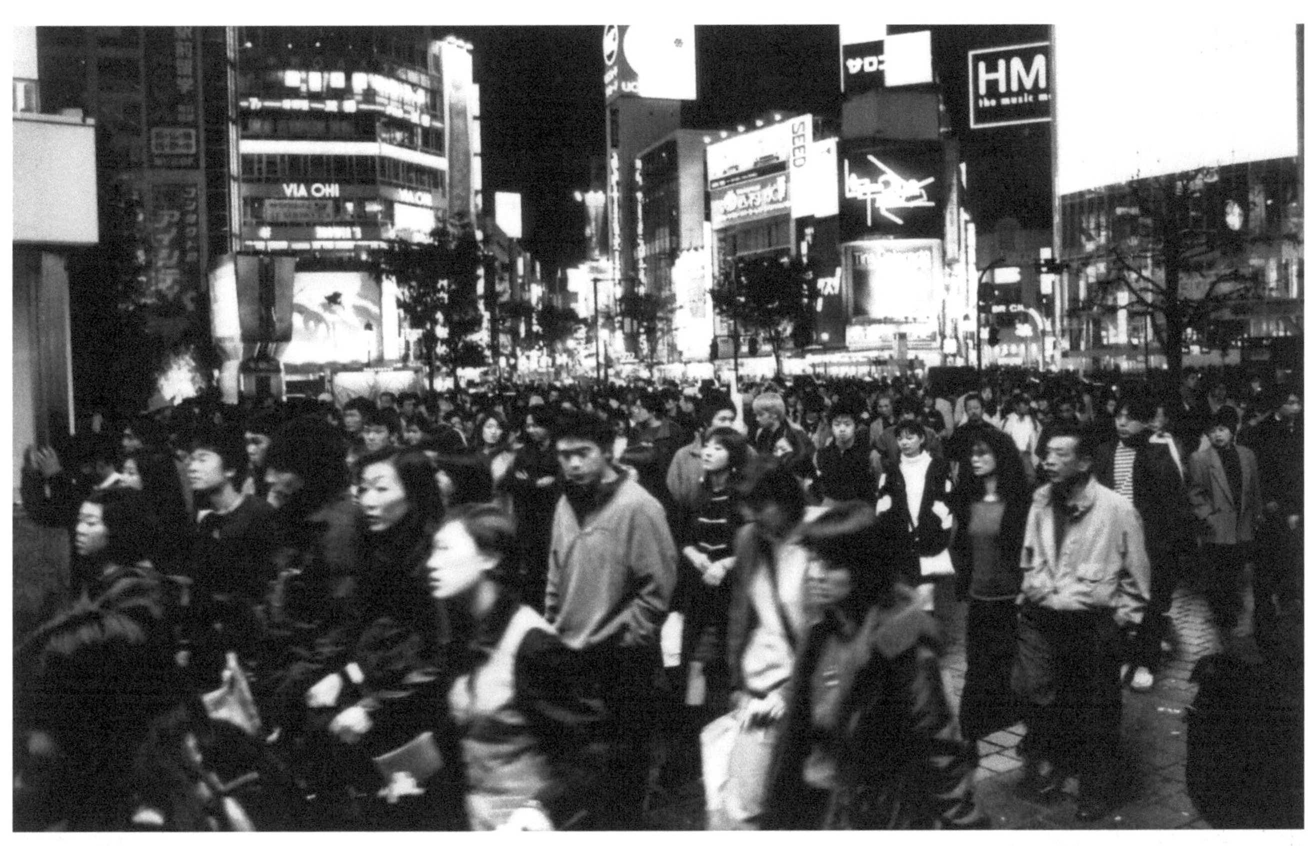
HM
SEED

places

The Great Buddha (Daibutsu) in Kamakura, Japan

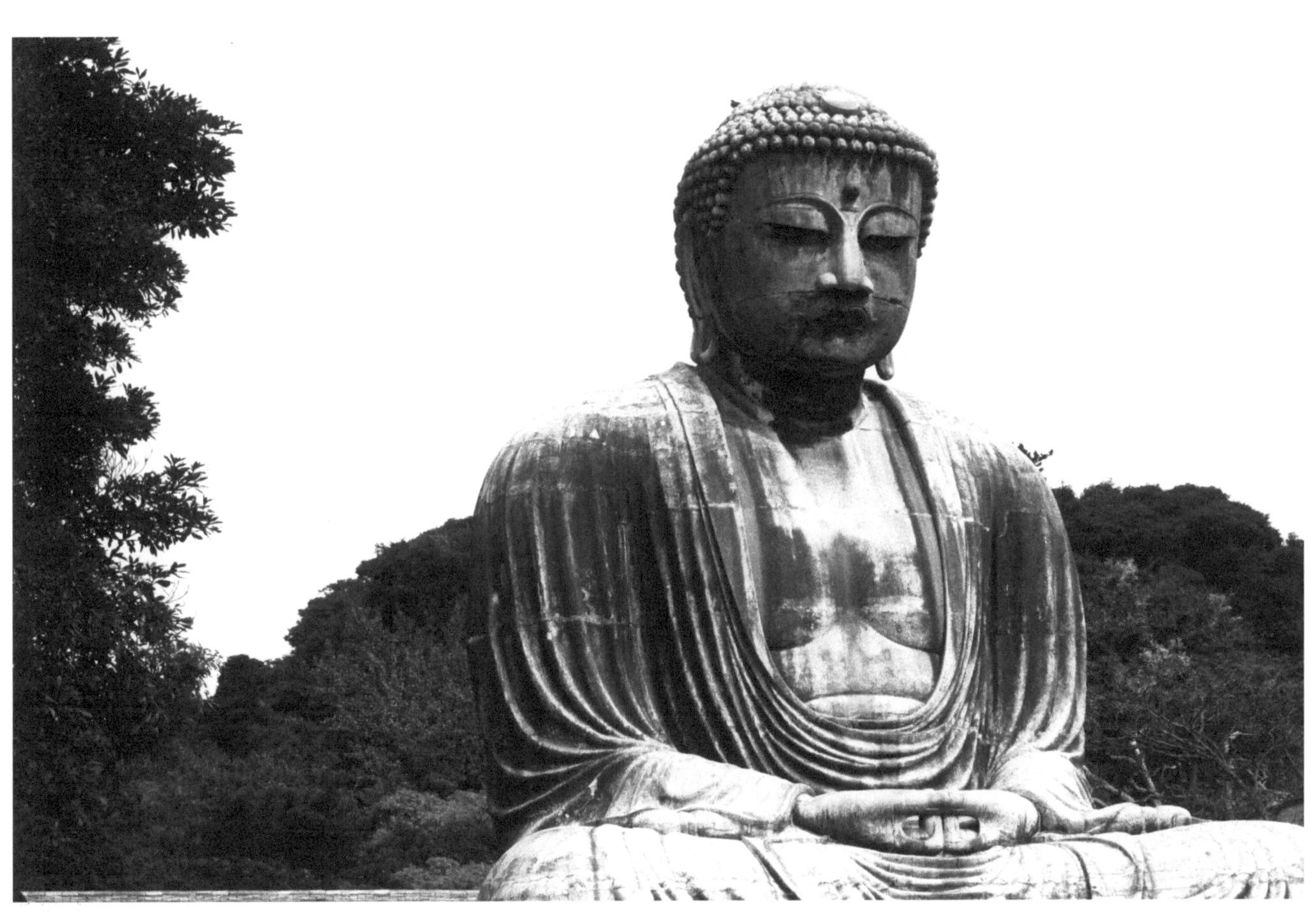

Little Buddha, Kamakura, Japan 1999

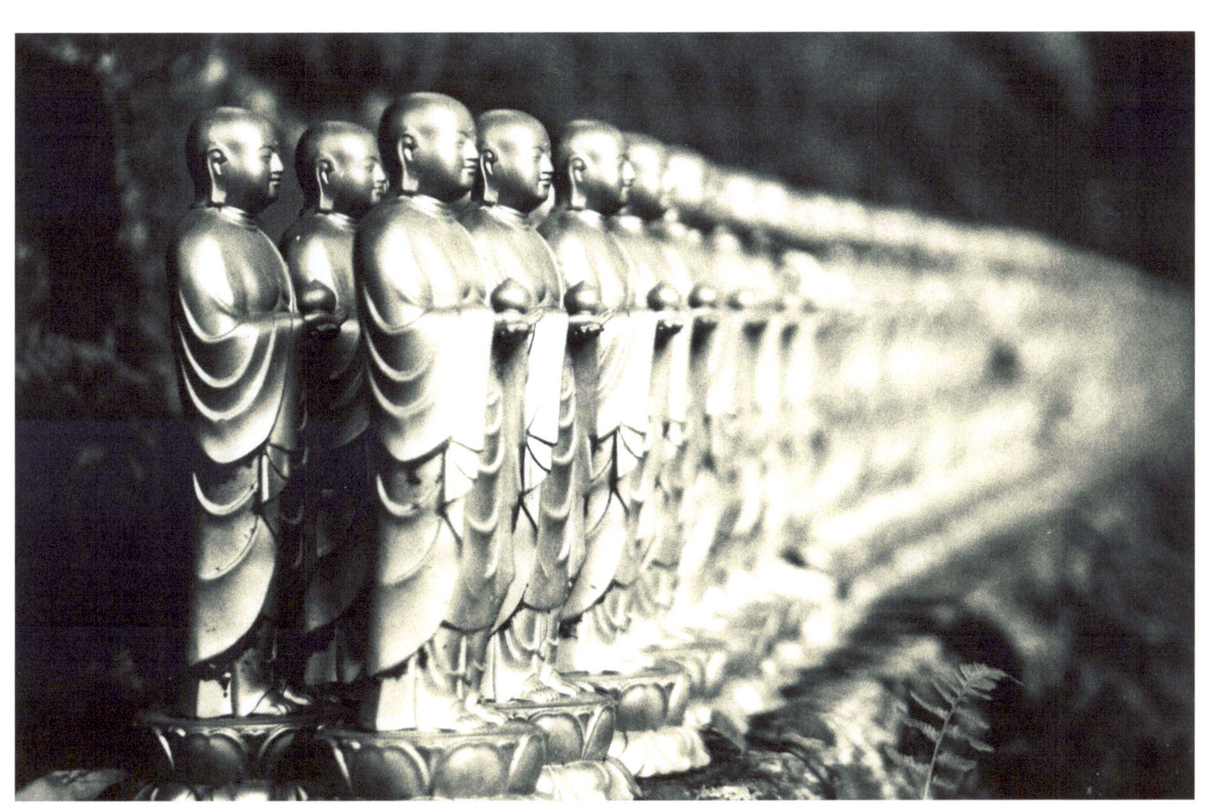

Temple Roofs, Kamakura, Japan 2000

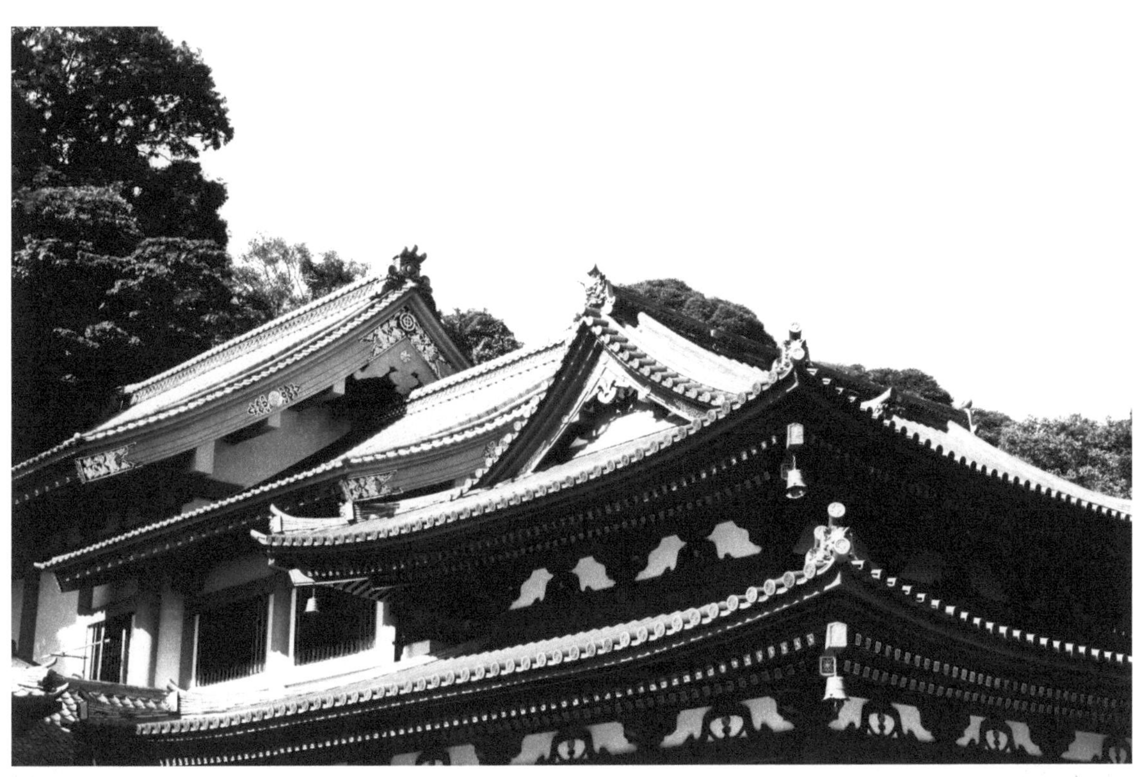

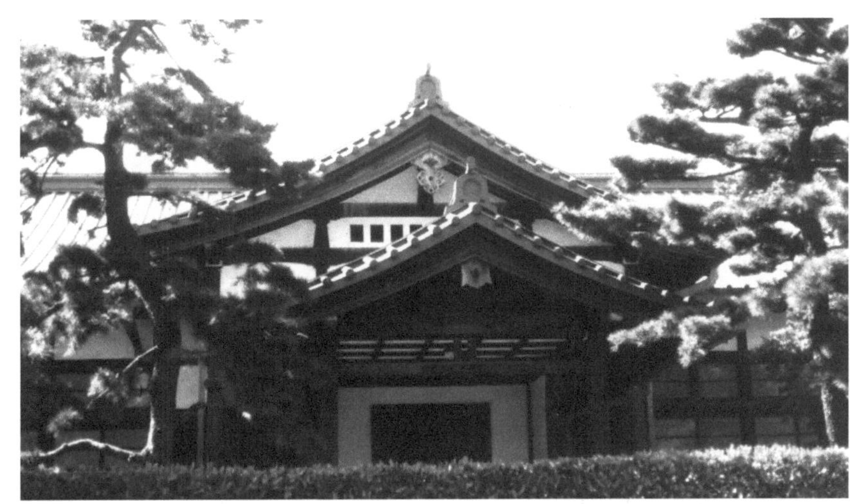

The A-bomb Dome, one of the only structures left standing after the Bomb was dropped on Japan in WWII, Hiroshima, Japan 2000

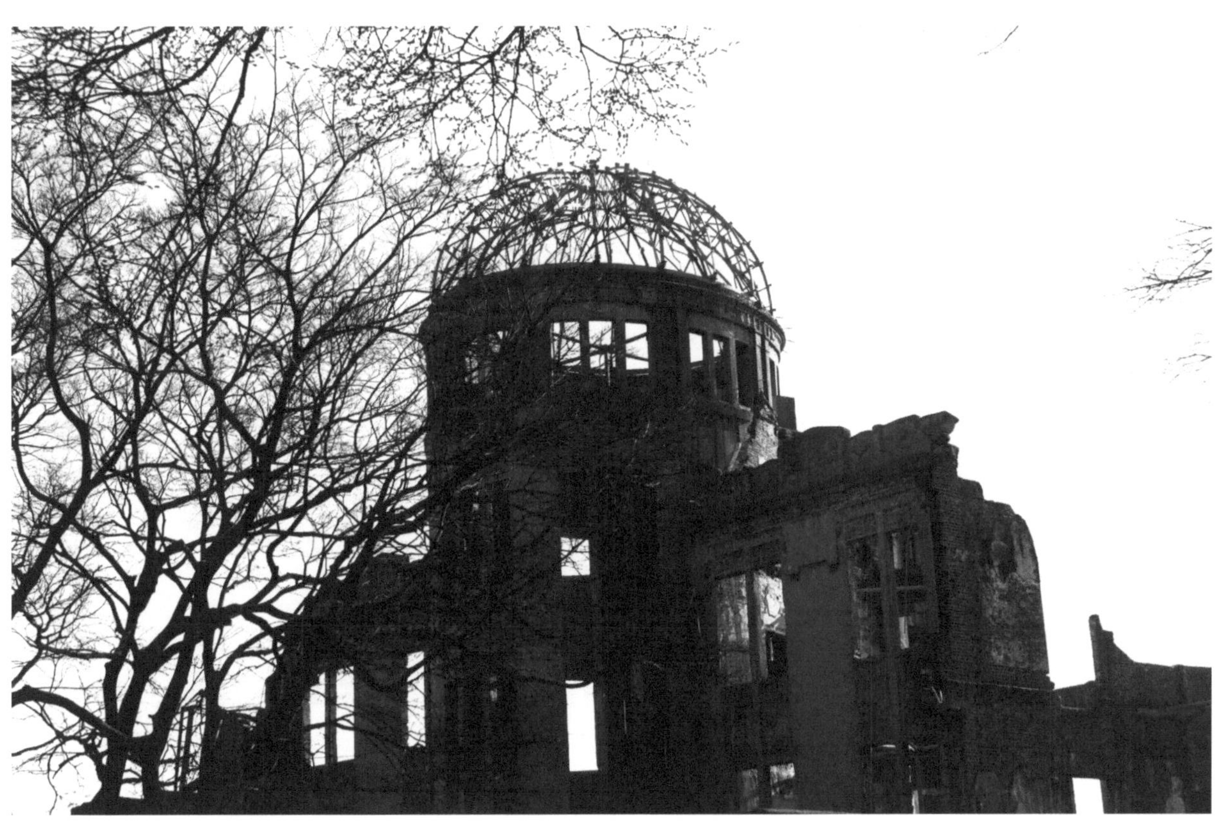

The Memorial Cenotaph in Peace Memorial Park, flowers are placed here everyday to remember those who perished on August 6, 1945 when the Bomb was dropped on Japan in WWII, Hiroshima, Japan 2000

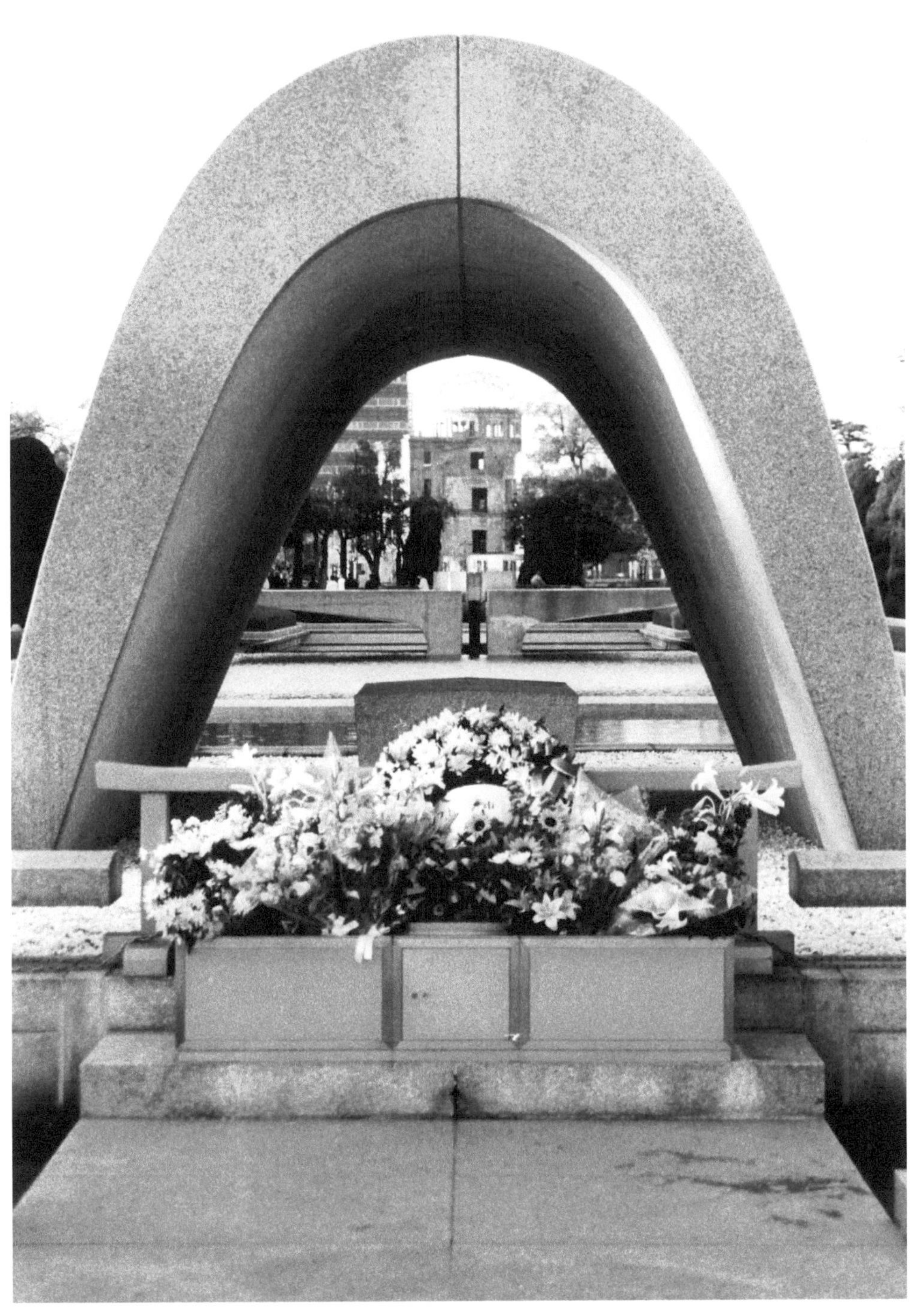

The Peace Bell in Peace Memorial Park, Hiroshima, Japan 2000

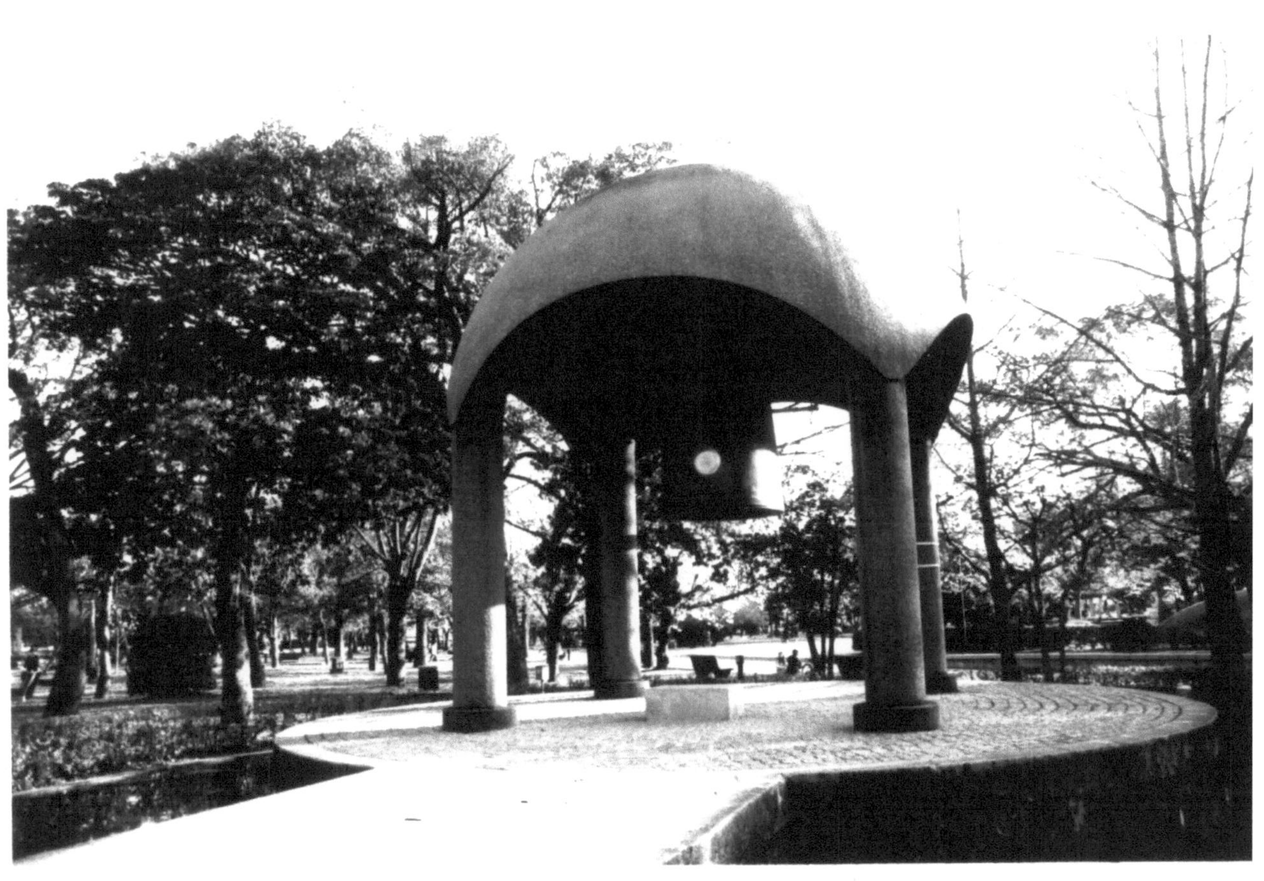

House on Victoria's Peak, Hong Kong, China 1999

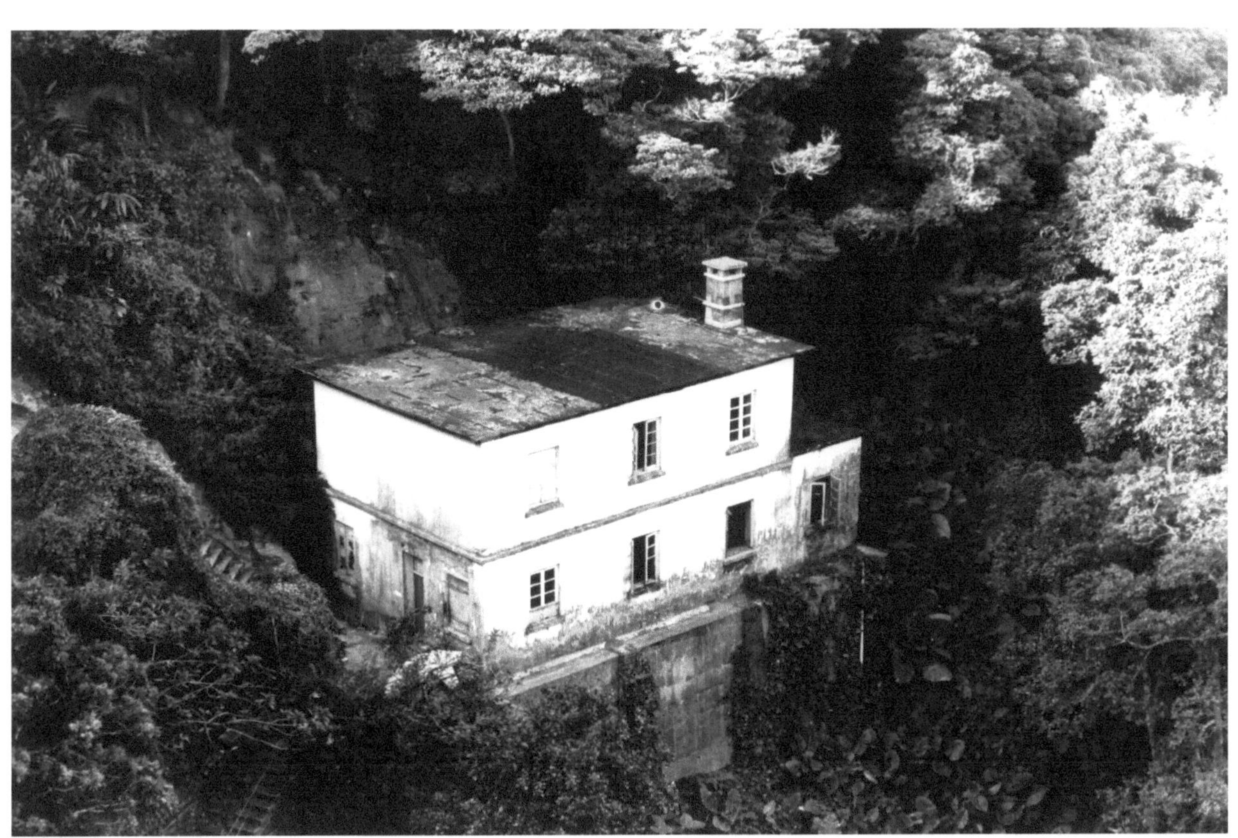

Windows, Hong Kong, China 1999

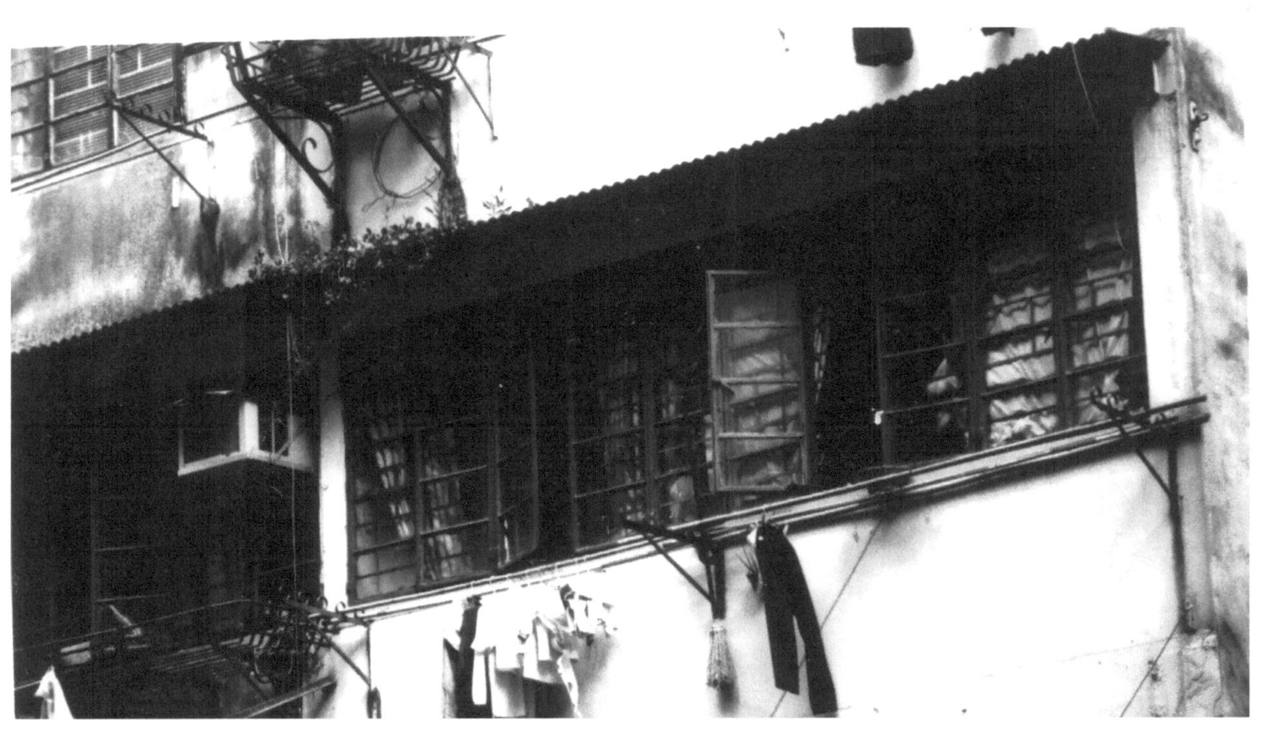

Downtown, Roppongi, Tokyo, Japan 1999

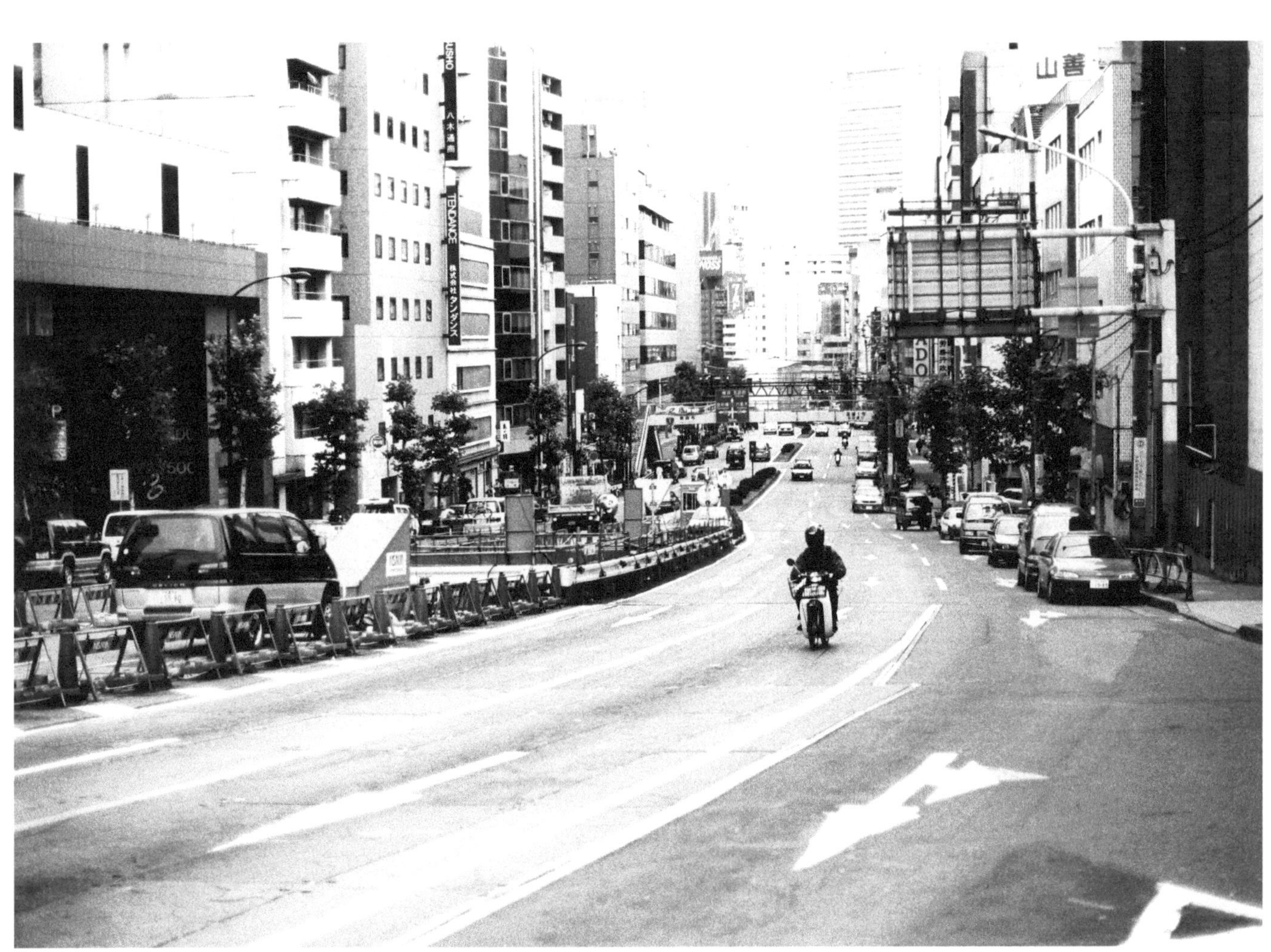
八木通商
TENDANCE
株式会社タンダンス
山善

Tokyo Tower I, (Japan's Eiffel Tower), Tokyo, Japan 1999

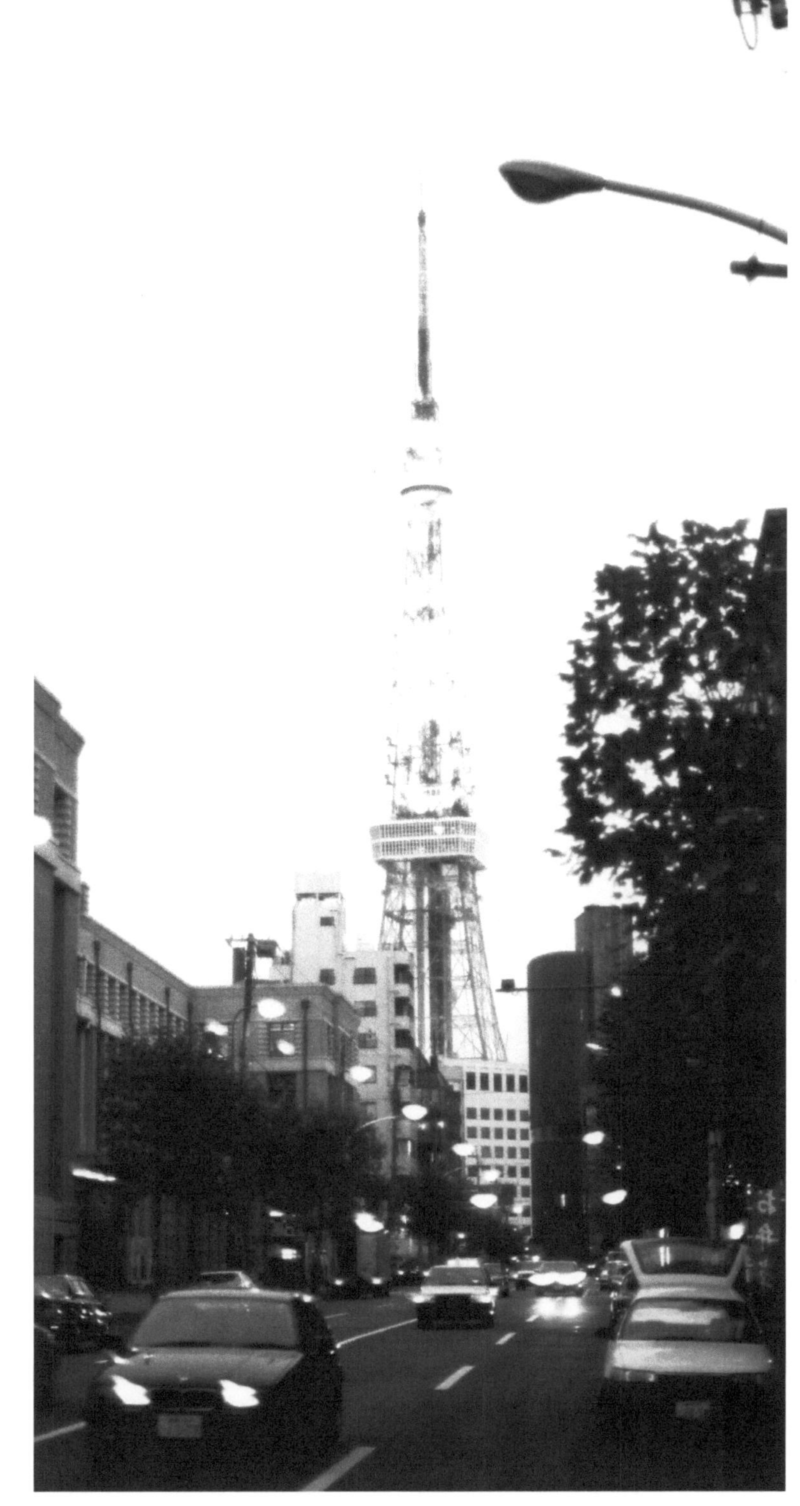

Tokyo Tower II, Tokyo, Japan 1999

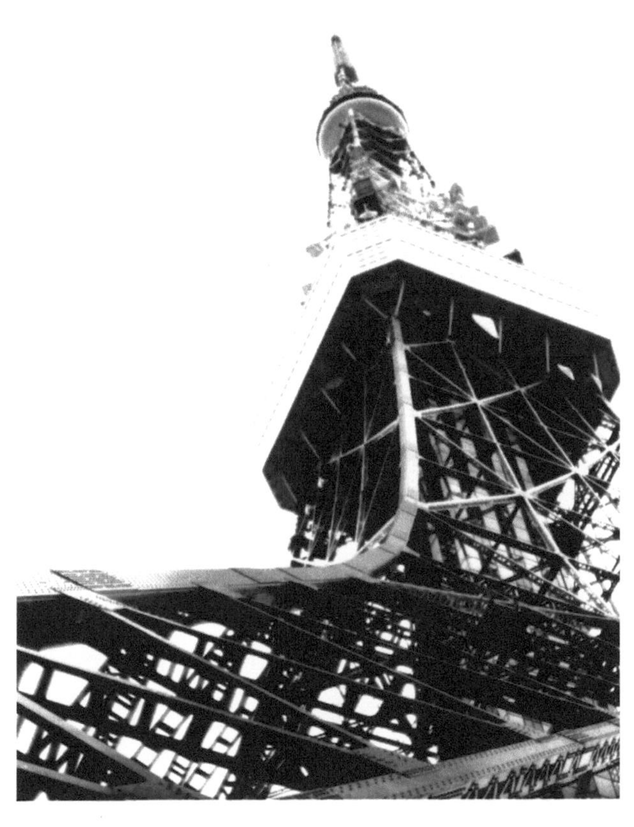

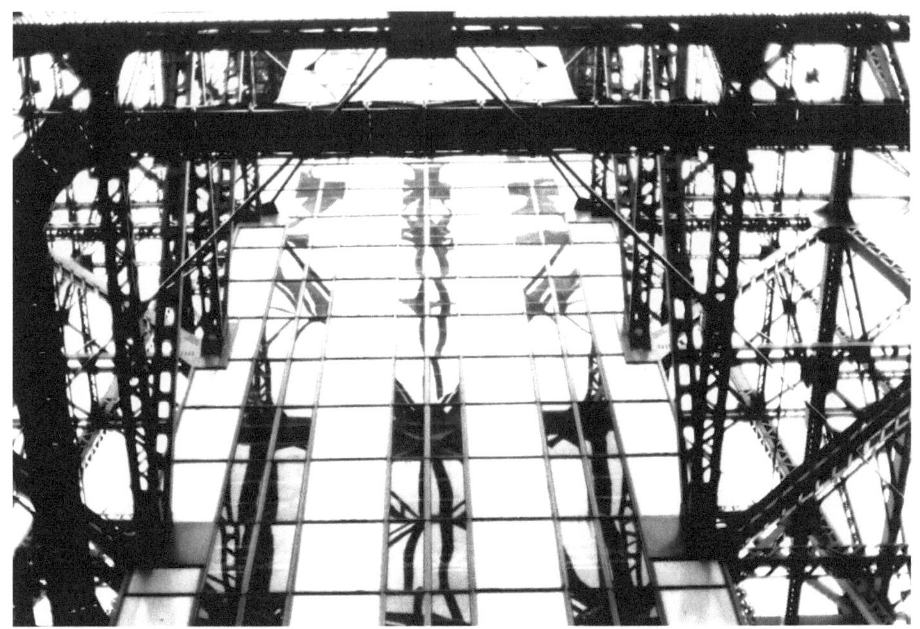

Downtown, Tokyo, Japan 1999

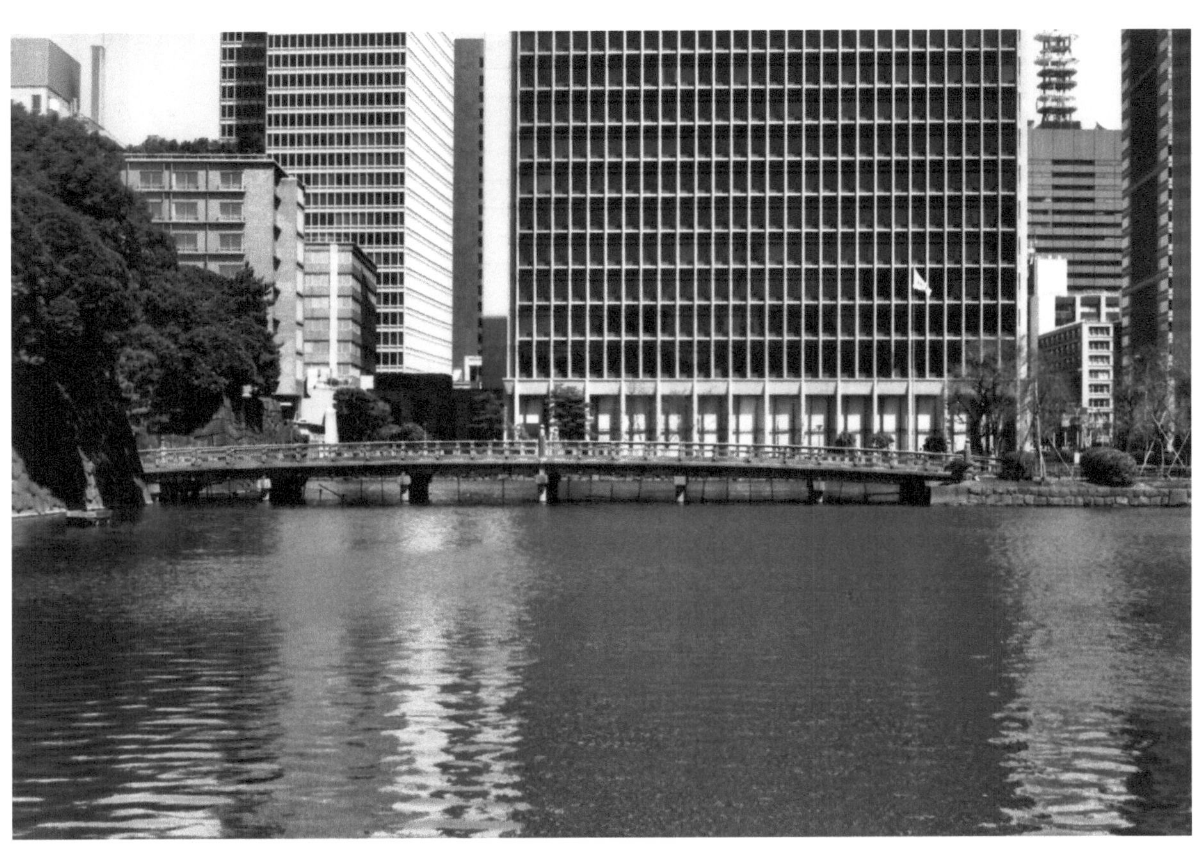

Skyline, Tokyo, Japan 2000

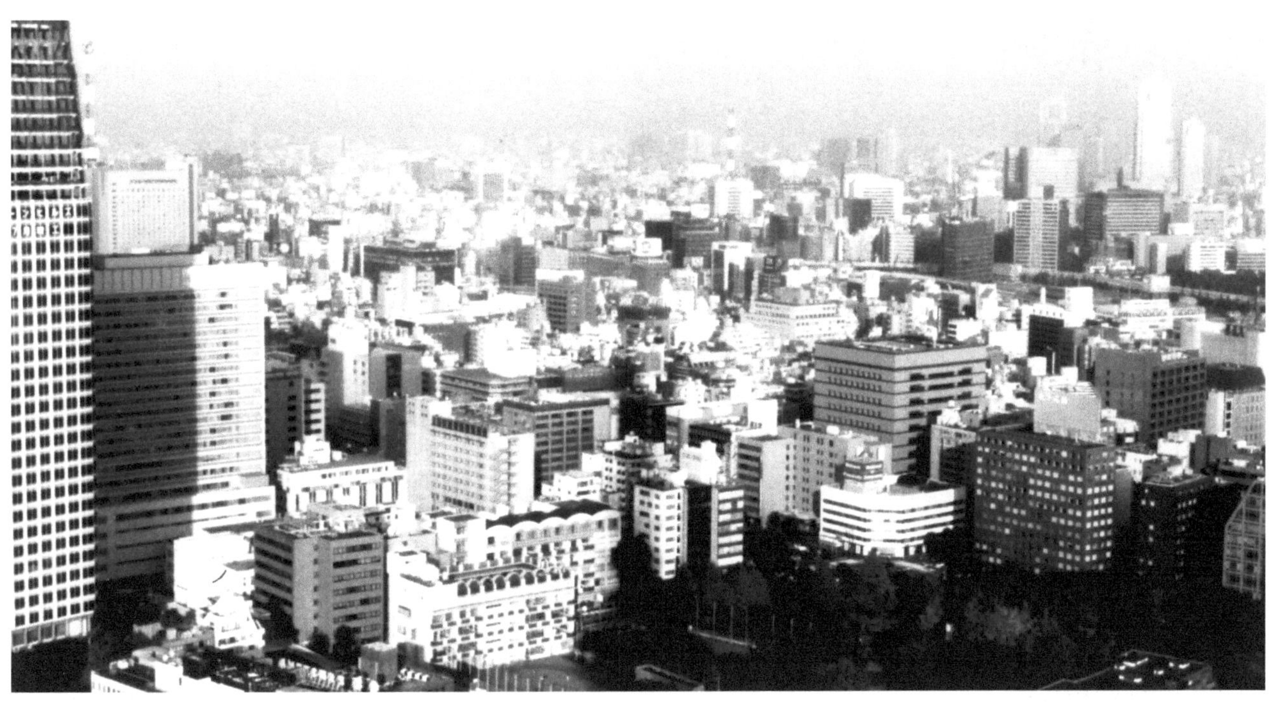

www.ingramcontent.com/pod-product-compliance
Lightning Source LLC
LaVergne TN
LVHW070144110826
845147LV00002B/323
9780615148342